ROME

centuries of stories of the eternal city

WADDLE THE WORLD WITH RED PENGUIN BOOKS

Copyright © 2023

All rights reserved.

ISBN

978-1-63777-537-0

978-1-63777-538-7

No part of this book may be reproduced in any form or by any electronic or mechanical means, including information storage and retrieval systems, without written permission from the author, except for the use of brief quotations in a book review.

Contents

PART ONE
ROME ...

WHERE ALL ROADS LEAD Vanessa Caraveo	3
ROME C. D'Angelo	7
MY FOUNTAIN WISH Hanna Swanepoel	11
ROME - THE GRITTY CITY Donna Keel Armer	13
THE BRIDE ON THE SPANISH STEPS Janet Metz Walter	25
PAPAL BLESSINGS Jim Tritten	31
NO KABEESH William John Rostron	39
HARVEY'S LULLABY Mark Andrew Heathcote	45
SOGNO ROMANO Annette Ermini	47
STAR OF THE SEA Linda Dickman	51
ETERNAL MEMORIES OF THE ETERNAL CITY Lois Schaffer	55
WHEN IN ROME, DO AS THE ROMANS DO Adrian Miller	61
THE ECSTASY OF CARMEL Rex McGregor	65

Running Through Rome   71
Stephanie Larkin

ETERNAL CITY, LASTING MEMORIES   79
Stephen deWolfe

AN AMERICAN SCHOOLBOY IN THE ETERNAL CITY   85
James Weems

LOOKING FOR A GREAT MEAL IN ALL THE WRONG PLACES   91
Adrian Miller

ROMAN HOLIDAY   93
Elaine Gilmartin

PART TWO
... AND BEYOND!

THE PARADISE OF A THOUSAND ROSES   103
Brian Jones

PERCORSO   107
Joe Farina

AMALFI LEMONS   111
Patricia Walkow

A DAY IN VENICE   123
David Lange

BAROQUE DREAMS   133
Joe Farina

All Venice is a Falling...   135
Joseph A Farina

KAREN (AKA GRANDMA) AND RACHEL'S ITALIAN ADVENTURE   139
November 2018
Karen Shaw and Rachel Abraham

PROPOSAL UPON THE RIALTO   155
Joe Farina

Meet Our Contributors   157

Part 1
ROME

Where All Roads Lead

VANESSA CARAVEO

Beautiful timeless, impossible Rome,
straddling those seven hills,
where legacy and nightlife meet.

Inspire me with your amphitheaters,
your colosseum, your squares and churches,
a place of centuries, of eons,
of history embedded in stone streets.

The Sistine Chapel, the domes of St. Peter's,
the quiet parks, the narrow alleys.
All the little spots in between
where life continues
from so long ago.

Mausoleums, centuries-old tombs.
Aqueducts. Brick-boned buildings.
That Mediterranean warmth and smell.

Marble and bricks and lush greens.
Modern restaurants just down the street
from the Pantheon, the ancient Forum.
Walk on and on and on.

All roads lead to Rome
but it's only when you get there
that you find yourself lost
in the sights, the sounds,
the entirety of culture.

People are so very human here,
so alive, so animated, so decorated
with the wear and tear of tourism
intermingled with their hopes and dreams.

What a place to wander.
Give me the silence of eons passing.
Give me architecture in its purest forms.
Give me, for a moment, Rome.

Rome

C. D'ANGELO

When I think of the trip to Rome that my husband and I took for our tenth wedding anniversary, my mind floods with images of architectural splendor while my mouth waters from the recollection of fresh pasta I ate daily, but there are some unusual stories that come to mind as well. See, this trip was a dream for me since I was a child. My grandpa was an Italian immigrant and when I was old enough to know what that meant, my interest was ignited and I knew I had to travel there someday to see the homeland. It didn't disappoint, and instead exceeded my expectations, which adds to why I love to write about my culture in my novels.

I have to admit, though, I was slightly worried about the time change and adjusting without jet lag when I thought about visiting Italy. I'd never flown overseas and didn't know what reality would include, from basic necessities to the true Italian culture in all its perceived beauty. Well, I was fine from the start in most aspects, including sleeping my normal amount of hours and time frame from the first night in Rome and on. I think my body knew I was home! But, my husband was another story... I woke up to him stirring that first night, with increasing sleep difficulty as the nights proceeded during our time there. He told me the noise of the city kept him awake, but somehow it comforted me. By the last night, I popped my eyes open to find his head out the window around 3 am, looking side to side with a confused expression on his face. When I groggily asked what in the world he was doing, he said, "Can't you hear the yelling? The cars?" I didn't, well not where it was disruptive since "yelling" is sometimes considered talking at a loud level for us Italians or Italian Americans. Despite feeling sorry for his lack of sleep, his exaggerated (to me) reaction to normal city noise still makes me giggle to this day—especially that head swoop. The poor man couldn't catch a break until our third city of lodging on that trip. At least we have a good laugh now about his unique ability to avoiding sleep for an entire stay in Rome.

Thankfully, the exhilarating experience of being on that soil fueled us in the daytime, from laying our eyes on the Roman ruins, the must-see sites like the Pantheon, the Spanish Steps, and the Trevi Fountain, to enjoying the foamy cappuccino and rich gelato soothing our stomachs. This Florida lady's first time drinking a hot drink without tongue-scorching was in Rome—it's always the perfect temperature in Italy. But let's get back to my husband, a man who's not as interested in art as me. I knew this fact beforehand, but didn't know the extent of it until our trip, where I scheduled maaany cultural elements. While I wanted to stare at every detail of a piece of art, building or otherwise, he glanced at it, appreciated it in his own way, and was fine to move on immediately. Accompanying me to museums, a selfless act on his part, led to his life-long insistence that ancient statues of torsos and heads can't ever be in the same room in museums. Oh, his love of culture runs deep, people. We'd walk into a room and he'd say "Oh, heads. Their bodies must be in the next room." The best part was that he was always right.

The last featured memory for me is how in all of our exploring in Rome we could never find Piazza Navona. I felt like we were in National Lampoon's European Vacation circling Big Ben and Parliament. How was a huge square that hard to find?

Well, this was before data plans on phones so we were finding our way everywhere by map and hope. At least we found a piazza (don't ask me which one) where bottled water was being given away due to the hot temps. In Italy, they don't just give out boring still water, though, it was sparkling—and refreshing after an hour's walk to find the mysterious piazza. We stopped trying to find it once the bubbles hit our throats and instead grabbed some cheese-filled ravioli and seafood linguine nearby to enjoy the night. Torsos, heads, and the Bermuda Triangle of piazzas were for another day and another eternal joke about the Roman holiday between us lovebirds.

Not only did our anniversary trip bring humorous memories and witnessing life-fulfilling sites to both of us (one of us more than the other!), we unknowingly began our passion of International travel. Oh, and we also learned each others' preferences a notch more than before this experience. I haven't packed in the sites on a schedule like I did for this vacation ever again, to my husband's gratitude. So I thank you, Rome, for laying the foundation for my husband and my worldly adventures. Luckily, they occur with much more ease nowadays, but still include welcomed silly circumstances we'll talk about forever.

My Fountain Wish

HANNA SWANEPOEL

If Rome was not built in a day
Or so they say,
I would imagine a glorious past
And everything would last
But in the myriad of walkways and historical
    buildings
Cathedrals and basilicas with all the trimmings
Nothing greater I saw
Spanish steps in awe
Making a wish at the fountain
I will remain
A while to sit and stare
Touring in my head
Paintings on ceilings and gelato instead
Pasta and pizza to share

Rome – The Gritty City

DONNA KEEL ARMER

Rome is gritty—2,774 years of grit. Everywhere you look, everything you see, every corner you turn, and everything you touch is layered with ancient grit.

Ray and I have been traveling to Italy since 1995, but Rome has never been a destination for us. We view it as a stopping-off place for the next segment of our journey to other parts of Italy.

Yet every time we stopped in Rome, we managed to stay a few days and knocked off at least one or two of the top tourist attractions. So far, we've crossed off the Vatican museums with the Sistine Chapel and St. Peter's Basilica, which included the good fortune to attend a service presided over by Pope John Paul. Also checked off the list are the Colosseum, the Forum, Piazza Navona, the Trevi Fountain, the Palace of Vittorio Emanuele II, the Pantheon, the Borghese Gardens, the Spanish Steps, and numerous other "must-see" tourist attractions.

But recently, we decided that we hadn't given Rome a chance to shine through all its grit. So we rented an apartment and stayed awhile to work our way through some of that ancient grit.

Our idea of big city living is to figure out how to make big into small. To do this, we picked an apartment in Prati on via

Crescenzio close to Piazza Popolo and settled into the rhythm of life in the largest and oldest city in Italy.

Most people know Prati as the part of Rome containing St. Peter's and the Vatican museums. During our stay, we came to know it as a beautiful residential area with lovely shops, restaurants, parks, museums, art galleries, churches, and obscure but important attractions rarely seen by tourists.

By giving Rome a chance, we were given the gift of some unusual off-the-beaten-track experiences. For instance, we had no clue that Prati is home to the *Corte Suprema di Cassazione*—The Supreme Court of Rome. Located in the Palace of Justice, this imposing edifice was just a short distance from our apartment. Locals call the building *Palazzaccio* (meaning the bad Palace) because there were so many rumors of corruption when it was being built. It was designed by Guglielmo from Perugia and constructed between 1888 and 1910. It is still considered one of the grandest buildings in Rome.

This architectural wonder is large (170 meters by 155 meters) —think much larger than a football field, which tops out at 91 meters by 49 meters. The building is completely covered in Travertine limestone. At the very top on one side is the coat of arms from the House of Savoy, and on the other side is a great bronze chariot with four horses created by sculptor Ettore Ximenes from Palermo. There are ten large statues of notable jurists, including Cicero and Vico. They adorn the internal courtyard, prepared to dispense justice at any moment.

Surrounding the Supreme Court is Piazza Cavour. On this rainy day, the calm, inviting park is devoid of people. With hoods pulled over our heads, we walk through the gardens, which date to 1895. In the center of the piazza is a statue of Camillo Benson, Count of Cavour, a famous statesman who was deeply involved in the movement for Italian unification. At the base of the statue are allegorical bronze statues representing Italy and Rome on the south, Thought and Action on the east and west, and Force on the north side.

The rain persists, but so do we. Our next stumbled-over discovery is a two-bell tower church built in 1911. It's called *Chiesa Evangelica Valdese*. It's a Protestant church—a rarity in this country of Catholicism.

Of course, we've worked up an appetite. Mama's Bistrot on via Sforza Pallavicini, around the corner from our apartment, was highly recommended by our hostess. Even without reservations, we are welcomed to come in from the rain and given a cozy table in the corner.

The feast begins. After all, this is precisely why we return to Italy year after year. The food, the wine, and the generous hospitality of the people entice us just like the sirens lured Ulysses.

Our lunch includes *Involtini al melanzane*—eggplant stuffed with prosciutto and mozzarella, draped with a luscious, velvety tomato-basil sauce. For me, *spaghetti carbonara*—pasta oozing with eggs, guanciale and pecorino Romano. For Ray—ravioli stuffed with lobster and shrimp. The grand finale—panna cotta—drizzled with strawberry sauce and topped with fresh berries.

Mama's, from that day on, is our favorite restaurant in Rome, so much so that anytime we find ourselves in Rome and it's time to eat, we'll be at Mama's.

On our stroll back to the apartment, we scout out *Cantiani's*—another recommendation by our hostess. It's a fairyland of takeaway food. We forage for our dinner with finger-pointing and gestures and come away with a variety of culinary delights to sample later this evening—another favorite place goes on our list.

After naps, an evening ramble, and an Aperol Spritz, we wash clothes. While we don't have a terrace, the living room has two large windows. We open them widely and position the drying racks just so to watch the last of the day's sunbeams zoom in on our clothes while we unpack and congratulate ourselves on finding this beautiful apartment in this gritty city of 4.2 million.

Each day, we continue our exploration of the Roman world right outside our front door. There's Hadrian's Mausoleum and the surrounding park a few steps away. We stroll to St. Peter's at night when the piazza is almost empty, and musicians on every corner shower us with sacred music.

We stop to watch children of all ages hop onto a carousel. Memories of sweet moments with Mom and Dad crowd my thoughts. I see them hoisting me on the horse's back and holding me tightly—a safe time in my life. Ray reaches for my hand. We lean into each other, listening and hearing the call of our childhood.

Our days are crammed with good things—things that dig deeper into the grit of Rome.

We explore the food and flower-filled markets. We wander through obscure churches filled with treasures. Our hands move over cool, smooth marble surfaces, spilling deep reds, oranges, and yellows into the waiting sunlight. We're surprised by the relic of Mary Magdalene's foot in a glass case.

The Jewish Synagogue and Museum displays ancient silks, liturgical and ceremonial textiles, illuminated parchments, extraordinary marble carvings, and works of silver. The Menorahs are works of art, as are the coverings for the Torah. There are mosaics with semi-precious stones and even a chair that says it was once Elijah's.

Across the street from the synagogue is Portico d'Ottavia, a complex of ancient monuments built in 27 BCE by Octavian (Emperor Augustus). A few steps away is the Temple of Apollo, dating back to 431 BCE.

Our last stop before a very late lunch is the Teatro di Marcello. We are thrilled that, unlike the Colosseum, there are no lines. This massive structure built by Julius Caesar in 27 BCE was the model for the Colosseum 83 years later. We walk among the ruins without crowds or guides. We examine delicately carved pieces of stone among the rubble. We move in a daze surrounded by historical grit.

The thing about Rome is that it's endless, and all roads do appear to lead back to this brilliant, gritty city. It offers endless possibilities depending on your interests. While our focus is on food and wine, we also love history, art, and music.

One evening, we combined all three by way of the Galleria Doria Pamphlj. Again, no lines and the freedom to wander unattended through the artwork, which is astounding—think Velázquez, Raphael, Titian, Parmigianino, Bernini, Caravaggio, and numerous other classical greats. We book a performance with a small opera company and are enchanted by Italian arias sung by talented performers in the Throne Room of Pamphlj Palace.

Our days and nights flow with the Tiber as we stretch our bodies over bridges to watch regatta teams practice in the autumn sunlight. We stand on street corners debating which gelateria is best. We discover our favorite place for *cappuccini e cornetti* at Franchi's. We hang out in Piazza Popolo and listened to American jazz. We window shop and consider a red Ferrari with a price tag of 1.4 million.

We are left speechless at the wonder of the light show of Julius Caesar at the Forum. We meet up with our Italian friends at Mama's, which has also become their favorite restaurant in Rome.

We find Rome's speciality of cacio e pepe in tiny trattorias. We sample supplí, deep fried and bursting with flavor, and margarita pizzas topped with basil grown in pots by the door. We partake of food so fresh that I often expect it to walk off my plate.

We search for and find bass markers on doors that used to be the homes of Jewish citizens. These markers pay homage to the Jewish population in Rome who, during WWII, were hauled out of their homes and assassinated in concentration camps. Ray holds my camera while I kneel and brush away the debris. It is necessary to remember. These brass markers can be found all over the world. For us, it's important to look for them.

We discover the Cloister of Bramante tucked off a tiny street called *Vicolo della Volpe* (Fox Alley). Donato Bramante (1444-1515), who designed this beautiful structure, was a great rival of Michelangelo. The cloister is connected to the Chiesa di Santa Maria della Pace, where Raphael's *The Sibyls* hangs.

And just when it can't get grittier or more off the beaten track, it does. And off we go again into a world of magic covered with a bit of grit.

This time, our adventure involves our neighbors from South Carolina. What we've discovered during our travels is that no matter how far we roam, there's always a touch of home just around the corner.

Stefano is originally from Italy. He and Anne have a house in Tuscany where they reside for six months out of the year. The rest of the time, they live in our neighborhood in Beaufort, South Carolina. They just happen to be in Rome visiting Stefano's family at the same time we're in Rome. The agenda isn't revealed, but Anne suggests we wear comfortable shoes and clothing as we'll do a bit of walking.

In the early afternoon, a text indicates they're on their way and will arrive around three. We stand outside the apartment and wait. Shortly after 3:00, another text comes: *there's a transportation strike, and the traffic is bumper to bumper—will arrive soon.*

Stefano double parks like all Italian citizens do. Culturally, it's important that the first thing we do is greet each other with hugs and cheek kisses. With that ritual over, we pile into the car. Having an Italian as the driver is an advantage as Stefano swings out into bumper-to-bumper traffic without a glance to determine if anyone will stop for him to squeeze in. Of course, they do.

Anne tells us we'll be exploring some Etruscan ruins. But first, we'll stop to meet the family. She follows up with an invitation to dinner at the castle where Stefano's brother lives with his family. Yes, you heard right—his brother lives in a castle. We are empty-handed, without a gift for the host and hostess. I'm mortified as it's bad manners anywhere, but particularly in Italy, not to show up with a gift.

I try to digest the castle news as we plow through bumper-to-bumper traffic. Anne explains that the transportation strike has forced everyone to drive instead of taking the metro. The normal twenty-minute trip turns into an hour. Finally, a sharp right off the main road and we plunge into total isolation. The car creeps through a tiny portal with only a whisper of wind between the car and the walls of the hamlet.

We are greeted by Stefano's brother and his wife (Claudio and Emma), the castle owners. There is no time for a leisurely greeting or a tour through the castle as an important event is about to take place: the round-up of a donkey.

What could be grittier than rounding up a donkey? How does one approach such an interesting task? When I inquire about the purpose of this excursion, I'm told the yoga instructor in the village wants a donkey friend for the donkey he already owns. Sometimes, it's best not to ask further questions.

Since we're all invited to attend the rounding up of one donkey, we pile back into the car and fly down tiny twisting roads until the car we're following pulls off into a wooded field and parks. We follow suit.

The yoga instructor is waiting for us. As the bravest of the group opens the gate and strolls into the field with ropes, I ask the yoga instructor for the donkey story. The translation goes something like this:

I already have one donkey, but he is lonely. I'm at work all day, so I've been searching for a suitable companion. I want my donkey to be happy, so I'm presenting him with a friend. I love my donkey, and I have room in my heart to love another. Each day, my donkey gives me a kiss before I leave for work and again at the end of the day. Now I will have two donkeys and two kisses. This is a good thing.

There is no satisfactory response to this outpouring of love and gratitude for one donkey, much less two. I've learned over years of traveling to Italy that the Italian people speak from their generous hearts. I am happy for the donkeys and the yoga instructor.

During the rounding-up process, I'm attacked by mosquitos

who are happy to "kiss" me all over. The donkey looks on with interest as we slap our bodies and jump around.

Our friends think the donkey roundup could take a while, as he has yet to let anyone get close. Anne and Stefano suggest we leave the rodeo job up to the experts and visit the Etruscan ruins, which are close by.

Back in the car, it's a short drive to a heavily wooded area with a crumbling wall. This area was once a city called Veio. It's located between via Cassia and via Flaminia. The Etruscans are an ancient civilization with unknown origins. The Romans eventually wiped them out. These Etruscan ruins have only recently been uncovered.

We trek down a faded path to an old mill with double waterfalls. The drop-off is steep, and the water flows swiftly, spilling over giant stones and fallen trees. We walk across the bridge and immediately step back in time as we approach ancient Etruscan caves. Ray ventures in but backs out quickly as the caves are dark, dank, and more than gritty.

A part of the Etruscan wall with an arched gateway still stands. Most of the area is fenced off because of the recent excavations. The discoveries date back to the Iron Age, with uninterrupted civilizations for at least 16 centuries beginning from the 9th century BCE. Posted on the fence surrounding the dig is an aerial view of the ruins.

As we walk back to the car, Stefano points out the bastion of his brother's castle, which is located in Borgo di Isola Farnese. The huge fortress-like structure is shrouded in the early evening mist rising from the valley below. Beams of sunlight filter through the shroud and create strobe lights across the red-titled roof.

We drive back to the hamlet and park in front of the castle. The small houses around the base are also owned by the family. Our neighbors Stefano and Anne are staying in one; his mother lives in another, as does his younger brother. In the past, these dwellings were the medieval houses of those who lived and

ROME - THE GRITTY CITY

worked for the owner of the castle. They've since been converted into beautiful attached homes.

We sit on the terrace of Stefano's mother's house and sip wine while Stefano and Anne provide information on the castle. It's unclear exactly when the history began, but well before the 17th century when Cardinal Alessandro Farnese bought the castle. It has changed hands many times.

Claudio and Emma raised their four children here—three are in England attending University, and one is in Yemen with the United Nations Food Corp—the parents are nervous.

The other interesting thing about the castle and the surrounding land is it's part of one of the routes of the Via Francigena in Lazio. This pilgrimage meanders from the cathedral city of Canterbury in England through France and Switzerland to Rome. The path crosses Claudio's land.

This is one of the most important pilgrimages in Italy. Each year, Claudio opens his land for the pilgrims to cross. They are welcomed at the castle, where they receive refreshments. After crossing Claudio's land, they continue their journey to the region of Puglia, where there are ports of embarkation for the Holy Land.

Claudio and Emma welcome us warmly into their home, which has been turned upside down because a film crew has been here making a movie (The Kingdom ~ *Il Regno*). The film crew only left yesterday, so most of Claudio and Emma's furniture and belongings are still in storage. This leaves the main living area devoid of furnishings except for a baby grand, oriental rugs, and a massive Renaissance painting.

The cavernous room echoes with the footsteps of time. The ceiling soars into hand-hewn rafters. A gigantic walk-in fireplace anchors the room.

We pass through the kitchen with its enormous six-burner gas stove, which Ray stops to admire. The large wooden table is covered with a bright blue and yellow cloth and groans under the weight of antipasti: juicy sliced tomatoes, a tray of prosciutto, culatello, and pancetta, a large wooden bowl of arugula, five different cheeses with a variety of freshly-baked bread and homemade marmalades. I salivate as the aromas circle the room and tempt my palate.

We enter the dining room, where a mammoth table is set for tonight's dinner. I count at least twenty place settings. It's clear we will be part of a large and joyous group of people. Crystal wine glasses and wine bottles line up on an enormous sideboard. A gigantic chandelier with crystal roping reflects the roaring fire, which crackles and pops as it chases away the chill of a cool autumn evening.

As we nibble and sip, Stefano grills sausages in the fireplace. The sausages sizzle until they burst open. They fill the air with mouth-watering aromas. When Stefano extricates them from the hearth, we grab the hot sausages almost before he finishes cutting them into portions. We're greedy for a morsel.

The taste doesn't compare with any sausages I've ever eaten—succulent but not fatty, roasted to perfection. I force myself to save room for the huge pork chops that are next from the flame—followed by Florentine steak—the best in the world (in my opinion).

Family and friends arrive, and the evening is festive. Laughter bounces around the room. Italian and English conversations tinkle against the chandelier. The story of the donkey is retold. Food and wine are continuous. We eat, drink, and talk until it's very late. The beautiful evening ends with wonderful fruit desserts and a homemade walnut cordial.

The midnight drive back to Rome only takes 20 minutes. We fall into bed with the glow of wine, friendship, hospitality, and fascinating memories of a donkey roundup and an evening in a castle. Tomorrow, Anne and Stefano leave for South Africa.

In a few days, we will leave for home, but not before we visit one of the major tourist attractions in Rome—The Trevi

Fountain. We never leave Rome without throwing a coin in the fountain to ensure our return to this beautiful city of grace and grit.

The Bride on the Spanish Steps

JANET METZ WALTER

Our first question when we were in Rome was, why were they called "The Spanish Steps?" The answer was that when they were finally built in 1723, after over 100 years of arguing over them, they linked The Spanish Embassy on the top with the Spanish Square below. Our hotel, as well as the Trinita dei Monte church, was on top. We were at the bottom, about to climb the steps, 135 of them, the longest and widest steps in Europe. There are three terraces representing the Holy Trinity, so some accounts say there are 174 steps. To get a little more confusing, the French commissioned the construction of the steps using funds left to the city by a French diplomat.

It was about 4:00 p.m., and it was hot. We were returning to the hotel after a day of sightseeing to rest a little before dinner in our un-airconditioned hotel room. The hotel was small, not a major chain. We thought it would be charming, and it was to some extent, but the promised breezes through the open windows decided not to visit us today. As we approached the steps, we saw what the crowd at the steps was looking at. A photographer was setting up his camera to take pictures of a bride and groom, who appeared at the top of the steps.

The bride was wearing a white organza gown with a medium-sized train. The groom was in a white tuxedo. All of the routine photographs were taken, hugging, kissing, dancing. Now, he needed them to come down for close-ups. What? She's going to come down 135 steps? Was the church somewhere down here?

A woman next to me heard me talking to my kids, who were 16 and 13 at the time. "No," she said. "The church is the one at the top of the steps. Very popular place for weddings." I looked at the bride's shoes to see how high her heels were. Fortunately, they were not high spikes but reasonably chunky heels.

Someone put her train over her arm to walk down. As she came closer, I saw that the bottom of the train was already showing some dirt streaks. That was nothing. The photographer took her train, spread it across the step she was standing on, and took several shots of both of them. I had no idea how often the steps were cleaned, but they were pretty grimy now, with the imprints of thousands of shoes spending the day walking on them. The couple turned from the side to the front. Someone adjusted the train to be coming down the steps behind her. The train was starting to look light grey.

"So I guess the ceremony took place already," I mused to the woman who had spoken to me. I couldn't imagine her getting married in that dress.

"No, the ceremony is at 6:00." She was apparently connected to the family or the church in some way.

"Oh," I answered with surprise in my voice. I wondered if the train was detachable and if there another one was waiting for her at the church. My husband, who had wanted to get to the hotel a half hour ago, wondered why I was so interested in this.

I understood him, but obviously, the crowd was just as fascinated as I was. "Because it's something new and different," I replied. It wasn't that I had never seen a bride get married outside or on the beach, but either she did not have such a long train, or there was some sort of ground covering for her to walk on, never mind walking down and back up 135 steps.

As the photographer started packing up, we started walking

up. My kids probably could have gotten up in a lot less time, but I was past walking up five flights of steps in school, and although the heat was beginning to wane a bit, I wasn't too eager to pass out on the steps or trip and fall. We eventually got to the top and looked at the church, then continued to our hotel to make plans for the next day and find a place for dinner.

The Spanish Steps have changed since this story took place. They are not grimy grey anymore. Evidently, they were not originally built too solidly and have been pulled apart and renovated several times, including in 1995 and in 2015 when Bulgari, who moved into the now bustling upscale shopping area, sponsored the 1.5 million euro renovation using travertine stone, brick, marble, and plaster.

In 2019, city administrators decided to "guarantee decorum" on the steps and passed ordinances against sitting, loitering, eating, and pushing baby carriages up or down them. There are still fines for sitting on them, dirtying them, or damaging them.

In 2022, two American tourists were fined for causing damage to the steps with electric scooters. Who knows how long they will remain white and pretty, but at least for now, the wedding gowns stay cleaner.

Spanish Steps - 2022

Spanish Steps - 1990s

Papal Blessings
JIM TRITTEN

While serving in the US Navy in 1972, many of our wives followed the ship from port to port in the Mediterranean. They found ways to entertain themselves ashore while we were at sea. My ship, the aircraft carrier USS Intrepid, pulled into Naples, Italy, harbor one bright and sunny summer day. I took a liberty boat ashore to the fleet landing within sight of the *Maschio Angioino* Castle, where my wife Kathy, daughter Kimberly, and Wini Coolbaugh, Kathy's travel companion, waited with beaming smiles on their faces.

"Jim, you'll never guess what?"

"What?"

"Kimberly was blessed by the Pope." With that, my wife Kathy handed me the following photograph.

I was blown away by what I saw. Finally, I managed to get out, "What's this all about? How did you and Kim get that close to the Pope?"

"While you were out at sea, Wini and I went up to Rome, right."

"Right."

"Well, as it turns out, there is a USO office in Rome, right next to Vatican City. We went there and got tickets for a papal audience, especially for military members and their families."

"Wow, how did you find out about doing this?"

"We stayed in a convent a few doors away. The nuns run lodging, and they helped us arrange everything."

"So, you just went to St. Peter's Basilica, and the Pope blessed Kim?"

"Well, it wasn't a walk in the park, but between Wini and me, we figured out what to do."

"Incredible."

"Yes, and the Papal photographer himself took this picture and gave it to us!"

I steadied myself as the enormity of the experience exploded in my brain. I looked again at the photo. Someone I did not know lifted up my daughter to be held and blessed by the Pope.

"Tell me more."

I put on the backpack that we carried Kim in while traveling ashore. We walked to the hotel Kathy had selected for this visit while she explained the details.

"The Pope holds regular audiences in Vatican City. One of the real treats is him blessing the children. Fortunately, we stood close enough to have one of his helpers take Kim from me and lift her up to the Pontiff."

I looked at the photo again. "Kim doesn't look very happy."

Kathy and Wini laughed.

"Well, I guess the blessing will fix that. After all, Kim got baptized on the Intrepid right before we left Rhode Island on the cruise." I thought back to all the classes I had taken and the forms I signed, all leading up to my permission to marry Kathy, a devout Roman Catholic. I had promised to raise our children as Catholics. Our daughter had been baptized in the chapel on the Intrepid, using the ship's bell to hold the holy water. We did the baptism on the ship because I was not Catholic. My sister Sue was not Catholic either, and Sue was to be godmother. The local churches in Rhode Island would not officiate the baptism. "Yup, I guess that'll make up for Kim having a heathen father and godmother." We all laughed.

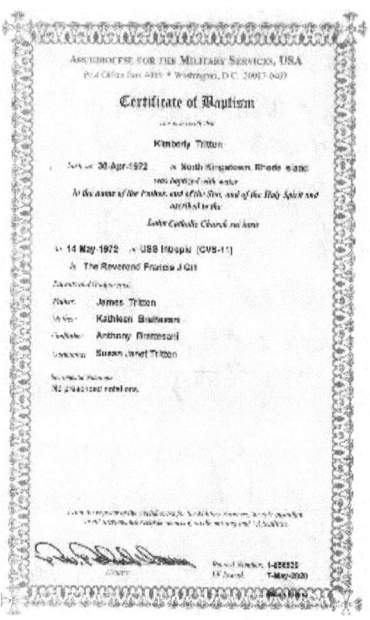

So, it was pure chance that my wife went to Rome and stayed in a convent where they knew about the USO center in Rome, which resulted in my daughter being held and blessed by Paul VI, 262nd Pope of the Catholic Church. Wow, could we top that?

It turns out we couldn't top it, but we could duplicate it. Some three or four years later, I was again in the Mediterranean aboard another aircraft carrier—the USS Independence. Kathy and Kim again followed the ship, but this time there, we had another child—my son James. Once more, when the ship anchored in Naples for an extended port call, Kathy met me at fleet landing. She informed me she had arranged for all of us to go to Rome, stay in the same convent, visit the same USO center, and get tickets for another papal audience.

After entering Piazza San Pietro, Swiss Guards granted us access to St. Peter's Basilica. Papal Household staff then ushered us into a vast indoor room. We could barely see the doorway where the Pontiff would enter. I wondered if it were possible to get close enough to have one of the handlers take my son and offer

PAPAL BLESSINGS

him up for a personal blessing by Paul VI. The crowd was large, and it looked like it was not going to happen.

With lightning speed, several things happened nearly at once. First, the door to our room opened, and the papal entourage entered—way off in the distance. The Pope was a small figure at the end of a sea of worshipers. Second, someone ripped my son from my arms, and I watched in horror as he was passed hand over hand by total strangers to the far end of the room. My son grew smaller as he progressed toward Paul VI. But he got there. I could barely make out his white coverall and hat as a handler took James and handed him up to the Pontiff. Wow, lightning can strike the same place more than once. I could barely see the Pope move his hands but figured he knew what he was doing, and my son had received a personal blessing from the world's most important Catholic.

In total amazement, I watched the small shape of my son as he was passed, once again, hand over hand, back in our general direction. I started to feel butterflies in my stomach as I wondered how the crowd of strangers would deliver my son back where he started. Unbelievably, he made it back to my welcoming arms. It must have been a miracle.

Another Catholic in my little family blessed by the Bishop of Rome, Vicar of Jesus Christ, Successor of the Prince of the Apostles, Supreme Pontiff of the Universal Church, Primate of Italy, Archbishop and Metropolitan of the Roman Province, Sovereign of the State of Vatican City, Servant of the Servants of God—the complete and official title of the Pope. It couldn't hurt, and it proved I had lived up to my pre-nuptial agreements with the Church.

The distances were so great and the action so quick that we did not take any pictures and never got close enough to the Papal photographer to ask if he had made a record of the event. Not to worry, the scene is forever engraved on my brain.

Bottom line, if you plan to visit Rome, visit the Vatican. It is incredible. If you visit Vatican City, get free tickets for a Papal audience, even if you are a heathen like me. Access for up to ten people can be obtained from any number of commercial touring companies or from the Swiss Guards at the "Bronze Doors" located just past the security checkpoint at St. Peter's Basilica. The USO Rome Center facility has closed, but the opportunity for a Papal blessing has not. Just "do it."

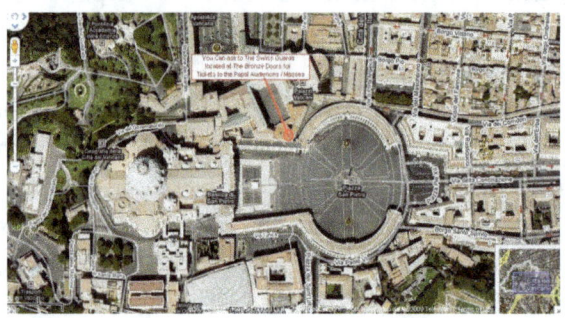

You can obtain tickets the day before the audience, after 3:00 pm until 7:00 pm (in the summer), or until 6:00 pm (in the winter). Check the Papal or tourist websites for the most up-to-date information or procedures for larger groups.

https://www.vatican.va/content/vatican/en.html
http://www.papalaudience.org/
https://www.vaticantour.com/papalaudience
https://bucketlistjourney.net/how-to-see-the-pope-at-the-vatican-in-rome-the-papal-audience/

For more information, contact the Prefecture of the Papal Household:

Prefecture of the Papal Household
00120 Vatican City State
Fax: +39 06 6988 5863
From the US & Canada: 011 39 06 6988 5863
From the UK and Europe: 0039 06 6988 5863
From Argentina: 0039 06 6988 5863

If you want to stay in a convent or a monastery, this can be an extra unusual addition to your visit to Rome. I remember the one we stayed in had a bar and served adult beverages. Consult travel websites such as:
https://www.monasterystays.com/?d=Italy/Lazio/Rome/Vatican-accommodation

No Kabeesh

WILLIAM JOHN ROSTRON

"No Kabeesh," was my only response. It had been a very long day, and I realized that my spelling and pronunciation were incorrect. However, what else could you expect from an (only) half-Italian-American lost in Rome? Still, I was rude that night, and I knew it.

We'd had a wonderful two weeks on one of those all-inclusive tours of Italy. Every stop along the way proved exciting and informative. However, the cathedrals of Milan, the Leaning Tower of Pisa, and the Canals of Venice had only been a prelude to the conclusion of our tour of historic Rome. Perhaps the feeling that we did not want this trip to end made my wife and I take off on our own on our last night in the "Eternal City." It was only then that we realized that our tour guide had sheltered us from the fact that we did not speak Italian.

Previously, every person we encountered spoke English. From the moment we disembarked in Milan at the beginning of our tour to that last night, there had never been a significant problem. Sometimes, it was a bit rough since our tour guide always thought we knew what he was saying even when his English pronunciations were way out there. For example, he went through a whole narration about the role of "Yipsies" in Italian culture. Was he referring to a uniquely Italian cult found in Florence? The thirty of us looked at him dumbfounded until someone determined he was referring to the Gypsy subculture that thrived in the area.

We had expected that our lack of knowledge of the native tongue could be a problem when we booked the tour. But we had two defenses (we thought) against any difficulties that might occur. First, our daughter spoke the language and was with us as part of her college graduation gift. Secondly, we had both been brought up in Italian homes.

Our daughter's language skills had saved us on more than one occasion. I especially remember the time we stopped at a roadside fast-food restaurant. In Italy, these places serve a full pasta meal at a place that looks remarkably like a McDonald's hamburger location. It was unusual for our tour guide to leave us to fend for ourselves. It made sense only after we realized that this stop was in an area close to where his latest flame lived. A lunchtime rendezvous had been arranged, and he had abandoned us to our own devices. That left my wife and me to decipher the lunch offerings displayed on overhead signs. Without our daughter, who had slipped away to talk with some friends, we were lost, doomed to possible starvation.

The five overhead boxes were labeled with the numbers one to five, much like a Chinese restaurant at home. All I had to do was pick a number. Simple, right? Not so when no one behind the counter spoke a word of English. I could not figure out how to say in Italian that we wanted *two* orders of number *five*, so I held up my fingers to designate my desire. Seeing the server put out *five* plates, I realized my mistake. I was about to get *five* orders of number *two*, *calamari* or squid, a food I distinctly did not like.

As I tried to correct my mistake, the server smiled and continued preparing enough squid to feed a small army. It was only my daughter's belated intervention that averted catastrophe. The server was more receptive when my wife and daughter decided they wanted the *calamari*. I stuck with number five—spaghetti and meatballs.

NO KABEESH

My second imagined defense against not speaking the native tongue was that my wife and I had grown up in Italian homes. Lol! All we had ever learned were mispronounced slang and a lot of dirty words. I swear it wasn't our fault. When my family had huge holiday gatherings (two dozen or more), ultimately, it resulted in the adults telling long, humorous stories and jokes. My cousins and I listened attentively as the teller went through all the details that made the story enjoyable. This would all lead up to the final climactic line—at which time all the assembled relatives would laugh hysterically—except for my cousins and me. The punchline was always a little (or a lot) off-color *and delivered in Italian*. What? After listening to the entire story in English, we were deprived of the reward. As they said in Brooklyn, "We wuz robbed!"

Of course, we had to know the meaning of these words long after we had forgotten the pretext of the joke. This was made tougher by the fact that the versions we heard of these Italian words were bastardized varieties that no Italian living *on the boot* would recognize. Before the days of the internet, it took me weeks of research (i.e., talking to other Italian kids) to realize that "fangul" had come from "bafangul," which in Italy was "Vaffanculo"…or "F*#k you" in English. All this is to say that my wife and I had no useful handle on the Italian language when we found ourselves lost in Rome on the final night of our trip.

With the planned part of our schedule completed, the tour members were free to choose our activities. Some decided to taxi to a particular place of interest we had seen during the day, while some found excellent restaurants where they could devour a five-course meal. Some, like our daughter, chose to rest and relax at the hotel. My wife and I decided to take a leisurely walk around our part of Rome.

We descended the Spanish Steps and threw three coins in the Trevi Fountain. Then, we enjoyed the ambiance of the buildings and the people and chowed down on the best gelato in the world.

It was late when we decided to head back to our hotel. The

streets were empty, and we assumed we had retraced our path back to the hotel. Wrong. We soon found ourselves hopelessly lost. Being the stereotypical male, I kept telling my wife I knew how to find our way back. It was always just around the next corner... until it wasn't. Finally, in all humility, I decided to ask for help. We saw a couple who looked like locals sitting on a bench. When I approached them and told them we were lost, I got an unexpected response.

"Non-capisce," was their answer as they looked at us quizzically. The phrase meant *I don't understand.* They were *too* local and spoke no English at all. I knew this from my brief research as a kid. They correctly said the phrase my New York relatives used frequently but mispronounced as "No Kabeesh." When my relatives used it also had the underlying current of being dismissive. It's more like, *I don't understand...and I don't care.* However, when this couple spoke the phrase, it was a sincere answer that they had no idea what I was saying.

Not surprisingly, we grew frustrated as two more individuals responded similarly. Confused about what to do next, we sat on a bench and tried to plan our next move. We were then approached by a couple a bit younger than us. They also looked confused and frustrated as they spoke to us.

"We're Americans, and we're lost. We keep asking people like you to help us, but none speak English. Do you?"

"No, Kabeesh," I answered. I had a smile on my face, but they couldn't see it in the semi-darkness. They turned to walk away just as my wife gave me a swift kick to the shins.

"Wait," I yelled to them. "Good news is we speak English. The bad news is that we are as lost as you. Asking us for help is like the blind leading the blind."

"Misery loves company," they said, laughing with us as we started to walk in no particular direction.

"So, you thought I was Italian. My Cippitelli grandparents are going to love you for saying that."

We walked along, joking and having a good time with our new

friends—wondering if we would ever find our way back. We passed by half a dozen hotels that were not ours, and they were all starting to look alike.

"I guess it's only the Italians who deal with tourists who learn English," said Sherri, our new companion.

"I think you're right..." I started and then slapped my head so hard that I almost gave myself a concussion. I had the solution, and it had been there right before us all night. "Every hotel we have passed by has a night clerk who deals with tourists all day long. All we have to do is walk into one of these hotels and ask for directions. We did, and it was so ridiculously simple that I was embarrassed to tell anyone the story.

Our daughter was already asleep when we arrived at our room, and we decided not to wake her. We didn't have much time to talk with her in all the rush and confusion of getting to the airport the following day. As we settled into our seats and began the transatlantic flight, Brittany opened the conversation by saying, "You guys were out late last night. I couldn't even wait up for you. What happened?"

I looked at my wife, and she let out a little giggle. I smiled at her, turned to my daughter, and said simply, "No Kabeesh."

Harvey's Lullaby
MARK ANDREW HEATHCOTE

Harvey, Harvey drives a red Ferrari
around St. Peter's Square.

Eating an apple or a pear
he really—really, doesn't care.

He'll drive it right around there, I swear
right around that great-big-Egyptian-obelisk

And park it just there.
'In the Centre of—St. Peters Square'

He's only 4 yrs old and free from the thrall
its tight bondage, that serfdom of prayer.

He'll sit and stare at its red granite.
And listen to his-own-little pomp-fanfare.

Like Pope Alexander VII
with brothers and nephews in-car-toe, coheir.

Sogno Romano
ANNETTE ERMINI

From a very young age, I held a deep fascination with Italian culture. I even knew I would marry an Italian-American—and I did. We met when I was a teen in college and have been together for nearly 40 years. Although we are older now, my sweetheart is still the tall, dark, and handsome fellow I fell in love with.

For years, we had dreamed of vacationing in Italy and took Italian lessons in preparation for our future travels. I delighted in every minute of our classes, thrilled to learn new words and pronunciations and string them together into lyrical sentences. I also loved the translation of my new Italian name, from Annette to *Annetta*, and my husband's name, from James to *Giacomo*.

Shortly after our lessons, we began planning our first trip. The research, booking, and anticipation of our visit were so much fun! It was 2004, and reservations were made the "old-school" way: via facsimile. I was so proud to fax my requests in Italian and took joy in receiving faxed confirmations in return.

When we finally departed for Italy, we had a night flight from Boston, stopping in London, then onto Rome, landing at the *Leonardo da Vinci* airport. All went well, and we arrived around 8:30 a.m. on a picture-perfect, sunny Sunday morning.

As we walked to the *pensione*, there was surprisingly little traffic, and the cobblestone streets were especially peaceful and quiet. The sound of church bells echoed around us, and a woman sang opera aloud as she strolled the Roman sidewalks, her robust voice reverberating along old streetscapes and ornate plaster buildings.

We settled in, took a short nap, then ventured out for exploration. It really didn't matter where we were going, as all roads led to Rome's Historic Center, *Centro Storico*, and all were exquisitely beautiful and awe-inspiring.

La dolce vita—the sweet life—was alive and well, as every corner and piazza flowed with the sights and sounds of sculptured water fountains and the scent of flowers in bloom. As we walked, we passed intricately carved churches and chapels and discovered quaint alleyways leading to mystical, enclaved courtyards.

Eventually, we arrived at a large rotary, *Piazza Venezia*, where a towering, central landmark stood. Nicknamed "The Wedding Cake" due to its grand stature and pristine white marble construction, it was built as a national monument to commemorate Vittorio Emanuele II, the first king of a unified Italy.

We ascended its massive steps, climbing up, up, and up again until we reached the crown of the monument and found ourselves on a wide, pillared rooftop terrace. We drew in a deep breath and looked out. As gentle breezes swept toward us, we drank in the most glorious views overlooking the ancient Roman forum and 16th-century structures from the great Michelangelo.

The panoramic vistas from this elevated height were an amazing highlight and introduction to the city! We later learned it was extraordinary to have this experience, as the top of the monument was only open to the public on *Primo Maggio*, May 1, otherwise known as Labor Day, Italy's national bank holiday. Our stars were aligned to be at the right place at the right time.

We continued our travels along an adjacent ancient road, *Via dei Fori Imperiali*. Normally a very busy and bustling street, all vehicles were closed off due to the holiday, making way for pedestrians and a charming array of street vendors.

It felt like a timeless, magical, infinite portal...

A classical guitarist's music wafted through the spring air. A Renaissance jester floated giant, iridescent bubbles with the wave of his hand. Another person set up a nostalgic gelato cart for all to enjoy.

Little did we know what was at the end of the road until we saw the majestic Roman Colosseum rise in the distant horizon. Wow!

While these were our first impressions on our first day in Rome, they continued to unfold as we wandered past ancient ruins, skirted spirited city Vespas, and, of course, enjoyed great Italian food and wine at romantic cafés.

Rome was everything I thought it would be and more. The element of surprise was everywhere we walked as we marveled at the magnificent art, artistry, and architecture at every twist and turn along the way.

It truly was a *sogno Romano*—a Roman dream—and a lifelong dream come true. I will always cherish this special holiday with the Italian love of my life, making our trip one I will treasure forever in this eternal city.

Star of the Sea

LINDA DICKMAN

For Emily Rachael

At the heart of Italy, in the City of Castles
a warm song was born
Embodied in Marietta Alboni
her very name meaning *Star of the Sea*.

Rossini favored her, trained her
toured this rare voice-among-women,
the deepest known.

Whitman, in love with Italian opera
fell deeply into the inviting waters
of her voice, vibrato, venerable
Queen among contraltos.

LINDA DICKMAN

The depths reached his very essence.
The heights wreathed him in light.
Her swirling notes,
spanning the length of a single word
lifted him
Giving naisance to a song of his own.

Eternal Memories of the Eternal City

LOIS SCHAFFER

Memories of a very special trip to Rome still resonate with me decades after my visit to the Eternal City. The year was 1968 and it was my first trip abroad. Just the thought of experiencing a different culture with people of different backgrounds elicited boundless anticipation and excitement.

My husband, David and I were born and bred in the United States. Two Jews who grew up in the Bronx. As we matured, learning about various cultures and traveling abroad intrigued us.

That reality was made possible when David was hired as general counsel at Avis Rent-A-Car, an international organization whose parent company was Chrysler. In addition to the opportunities to visit various parts of the world, our travels also initiated friendships with people within the United States and abroad. It is interesting to note that we have maintained some of those friendships to this day.

The purpose of this trip was to attend an international Avis convention that would connect us socially and professionally with Europeans and people from different parts of the United States.

Prior to our departure we had dinner with a friend and told him about our upcoming trip.

Our friend listened and delightedly he explained, "A Roman friend of mine is a Jesuit priest who can arrange for a Papal audience." He quickly added, "It doesn't mean a private audience, but one that is in the Basilica that the Pope conducts about twice a week with hundreds of people in attendance."

"Sounds great, anyway," we said.

Neither smartphones, nor computers existed in the 60's, consequently our friend reached into his jacket and took out his pen and a piece of paper, as he continued to speak, "I'll be in touch with my friend and tell him to expect your call when you arrive. This is his phone number," he said as he wrote down the information and handed it to us.

We called the priest upon our arrival and met with him at a church in the heart of a lovely neighborhood in Rome.

The priest was an elderly tall, lean man with sparkling blue eyes. Our conversation was made easy by his excellent command of English. We chatted for a while and shared how we just happened to have dinner with our mutual friend and how grateful we were that he had connected us to the priest.

Without further ado, he said, "I have six tickets," and inserted them into an envelope. "Present them when you arrive at the Basilica and someone will direct you to your seats.

After thanking the priest profusely, David and I walked out of the church and hailed a taxi back to our hotel. We felt as though our feet weren't touching the ground, so enthralled were we at our good fortune.

"Remarkable," David exclaimed, as we rode in the taxi. "Six tickets!" Now, who can we invite to join us?"

"Good question. Who can we ask that would be most appropriate?"

David thought for a moment. "What about Ron?"

"Good idea," I said, "because he is also a Jew and I think would especially appreciate experiencing this opportunity. Who else do you think we can include?"

"How about Keith?"

"Keith," of course.

Keith was a young London resident and Avis' financial advisor. David and Keith had a lot in common due to their legal and financial backgrounds. "He would be thrilled to attend the audience," David added.

Then David blurted out, "The two Irishmen, Mike and Sean."

"That's a super idea."

"Let's go find those guys and invite them," David said, the minute the taxi dropped us off at our hotel.

Later we learned that Chrysler was also distributing tickets for the audience. However, there was a caveat. Those who would be eligible to secure a ticket had to be part of the Chrysler/Avis organizational upper echelon and Catholic.

While Mike and Sean were Catholic, they did not qualify because they were not included in the organization's upper rank.

The rest of us fit neither category.

I vividly recall the six of us arriving at St. Peter's at the Basilica. The first glimpse of the building in all its overpowering beauty, the grandeur and vastness left us speechless. Soon we were ushered to our seats close to where the Pope would deliver his address.

As we waited for the service to begin, we kept smiling at one another. It was almost as if we knew what each of us was thinking. It was a communal disbelief that we were having such a momentous experience.

We then noticed a large group of people entering the nave. It was the Chrysler/Avis contingent comprised of both corporation's Catholics and upper echelon employees.

We watched as they approached us, nodded in recognition and observed as they continued walking all the way to the back of the nave.

Later we learned that the seating in the Basilica was determined by one's importance. It was the Jesuit priest who had made it possible for our seating up front. David and I chuckled that here we were two Jews from the Bronx who had managed to secure better seats than the big shots.

While Ron and Keith derived a special feeling from this experience, Mike and Sean were over the moon. They could not stop hugging us after the service was over and practically davened whenever they saw us in endless genuine gratitude for having made it possible for them to see the Pope.

More than fifty years have elapsed since that memorable day. I've never forgotten the joy we felt and our added pleasure making it possible for others to have this unforgettable experience. I've always wondered whether that experience still resonates with those who accompanied us on that day, particularly Mike and Sean as it does with David and me.

When in Rome, Do as the Romans Do

ADRIAN MILLER

I love to eat. Needless to say, Rome is one of my favorite cities in Europe. I mean, the art and architecture, the history, ruins, and churches, and, oh yes, the food. The glorious, difficult-to-compare food that made me plot my day's wanderings with an eye to where I wanted to eat at night. An out-of-the-way restaurant? No matter. One can find art, churches, and scenic wonders pretty much everywhere in this glorious city.

And so, one cold night in February, I found myself wandering on a quiet street toward a wine bar and restaurant recommended by a contact in New York.

Walking quickly in acknowledgment of the "brisk" weather, I made my way to my destination and walked right in. There wasn't a sound, and I assumed that the "hordes" of diners would be in another room in the restaurant. My assumption was...wrong. I was the ONLY guest in the restaurant, and once more, I assumed that I was just too early, even though it was 8:30 p.m., a perfectly acceptable time to dine in Rome. And so, seeing as it was also a wine bar, I ordered a glass of red and told the wait staff I'd sit for a while before ordering. Thirty minutes, then forty-five, and still no one showed up. By that point, I was done with my wine and definitely uncomfortable. I paid my check and went out to the street, feeling light-headed due to the combination of wine and a lack of food. And so, I decided to follow folks who "looked" like they were headed to dinner. Couples, groups of four, walking with a decidedly definitive gait and looking like they knew just where they were going. And so they did. We arrived at a brightly lit local restaurant on one of those back streets that seemingly only "locals" know. Entering the restaurant, I was greeted with a kiss on each cheek, shown to a cozy table that afforded me great people-watching, and with a few tips from the affable waiter, I ordered what turned out to be one of the best meals of my life. Reasonably priced and served with pleasure, my evening, which started out without much of a glimmer of hope, turned out to be one of the best of this trip. As they say: when in Rome do as the Romans do. I'd add, eat where the Romans eat.

The Ecstasy of Carmel
REX MCGREGOR

Back at home, her mother prayed Carmel would meet "a nice Catholic boy" in Italy.

"I'm twenty-seven, Mum. I'm past boys."

"A nice Catholic man, then. Or a nice Catholic Martian. A nice Catholic anything."

On the tour's free day in Rome, Carmel skipped the excursion to Hadrian's Villa.

"I need a break. After being herded through the Colosseum and crammed into the Sistine Chapel, I'm fed up with jabbering tourists."

She set off to explore a quieter part of the city on her own.

Around noon, she stopped for a rest in a tiny church. The only other person there was a young man staring intently at the ceiling. Carmel's gaze automatically drifted upwards. She was looking at some sort of dome.

"Are you a Borromini fan, too?" the man asked.

"Pardon?"

"I'm sorry. This church is off the beaten track. I assumed you were here to admire the architecture."

"No, no. I just popped in out of the blue."

"Well, fate has led you to San Carlo alle Quatro Fontane. An absolute gem."

Amongst a torrent of details, she heard him say, "Borromini's crypt is here. It's still empty because he committed suicide. We aren't allowed in. But then, neither is he. There was a long-standing rivalry between him and Bernini. They both had talent. But Bernini had charm. So, guess who got the commissions."

"Bernini."

"Correct."

Carmel felt like a television quiz show contestant winning a million dollars for naming the days of the week. She recalled a fact from yesterday's tour. "Didn't he design the colonnade in St. Peter's Square?"

"Correct again. His works are all over the place. Actually, two of them are next on my list. One's virtually next door. And his absolute masterpiece is just a couple of blocks away. Would you care to join me?"

"Sure."

At Sant'Andrea, after he raved about this "pearl of the Baroque," Carmel watched him light a candle. The gesture may simply have been a tribute to the architect. Or it could mean that he was... "Guess what, Mum."

Outside, at the first intersection they came to, he asked, "Remember the obelisk in St. Peter's Square?"

"Yeah. It was... tall."

"You can view three more from this very spot. The Esquiline way over there in front of Santa Maria Maggiore. See it?"

"Uh-huh."

"Now, turn to your right. The Quirinale. And to your right again, the Trinità."

Sure enough, three giant obelisks stood out in the distance, perfectly aligned and visible together, only from this one magical vantage point Carmel shared with her fascinating stranger. She was utterly overwhelmed.

More was to come. Bernini's "absolute masterpiece" turned

out to be not a church but an artwork inside one. The church was Santa Maria della Vittoria, and the sculpture was *The Ecstasy of Saint Teresa*.

Watching the saint writhe in orgasmic joy as an angel pierced her heart with the arrow of divine love, Carmel felt a distinct stirring within her own heart. Could this really be happening so fast?

Over the next few days, she visited more churches with Geoff. He always lit a candle. Each one was a tiny flame, but cumulatively, they seemed to spread like wildfire and set Carmel's heart ablaze.

She sent a postcard home:

"Hi, Mum. Italy is heaven. I'm having the understatement of my life. Love, Carmel.

P.S. Remember you prayed I'd meet a nice Catholic guy? Well, you should never underestimate the power of prayer."

By the end of the week, Carmel's future was settled. She would return home, quit her job, and fly to Vancouver to be with Geoff.

On their last day in Rome, he took her up the Capitoline Hill for a farewell view of the Forum.

"One more treat," he said, guiding her to the top of a steep cliff. "This is the Tarpeian Rock. Have you heard of it?"

"Nope." Carmel felt confident enough to admit her ignorance now. She knew Geoff relished enlightening her.

"It was a place of execution. The ancient Romans used to throw traitors to their death. Whenever I look down there, I picture broken bodies. Skulls smashed. Limbs contorted into weird angles."

Carmel chuckled. "I'm not seeing it. Guess I'm just too happy."

"You win," said Geoff. "I'll keep my gruesome mouth shut."

"No. Don't stop. I love hearing you ramble on."

He kissed her to show he enjoyed her teasing. "Oh, I ramble on, do I?"

"Didn't you realize?"

"Believe it or not, I'm usually hopeless at opening up."

"You must have a hard time at Confession."

"Confession? What do you think I am? Catholic or something?"

Carmel gasped. "The... the candles..."

"Oh, that. I just like lighting them. Get a real buzz out of it. I suspect I'm a low-level pyromaniac. But at least I'm not some religious nutter. I despise that nonsense. Think of all the great artists over the centuries forced to bend their genius in the service of Christian fairy tales. How else could they earn a crust? I don't blame the Church back then. It acted in accordance with the prevailing wisdom of the time. What bugs me is anyone still falling for that guff, knowing what we know now. Naivety won't wash as an excuse anymore. In this day and age, religion is sheer hypocrisy."

He leaned over the railing with his arms outstretched. "Viva science! Viva truth!"

He was so precariously balanced that a slight nudge from Carmel would send him tumbling down to certain death. If anyone were watching, it would look like she was trying to save him.

Unfortunately, the Sixth Commandment states, "Thou shalt not kill."

So she simply walked away.

When in Rome, you can't always do as the Romans did.

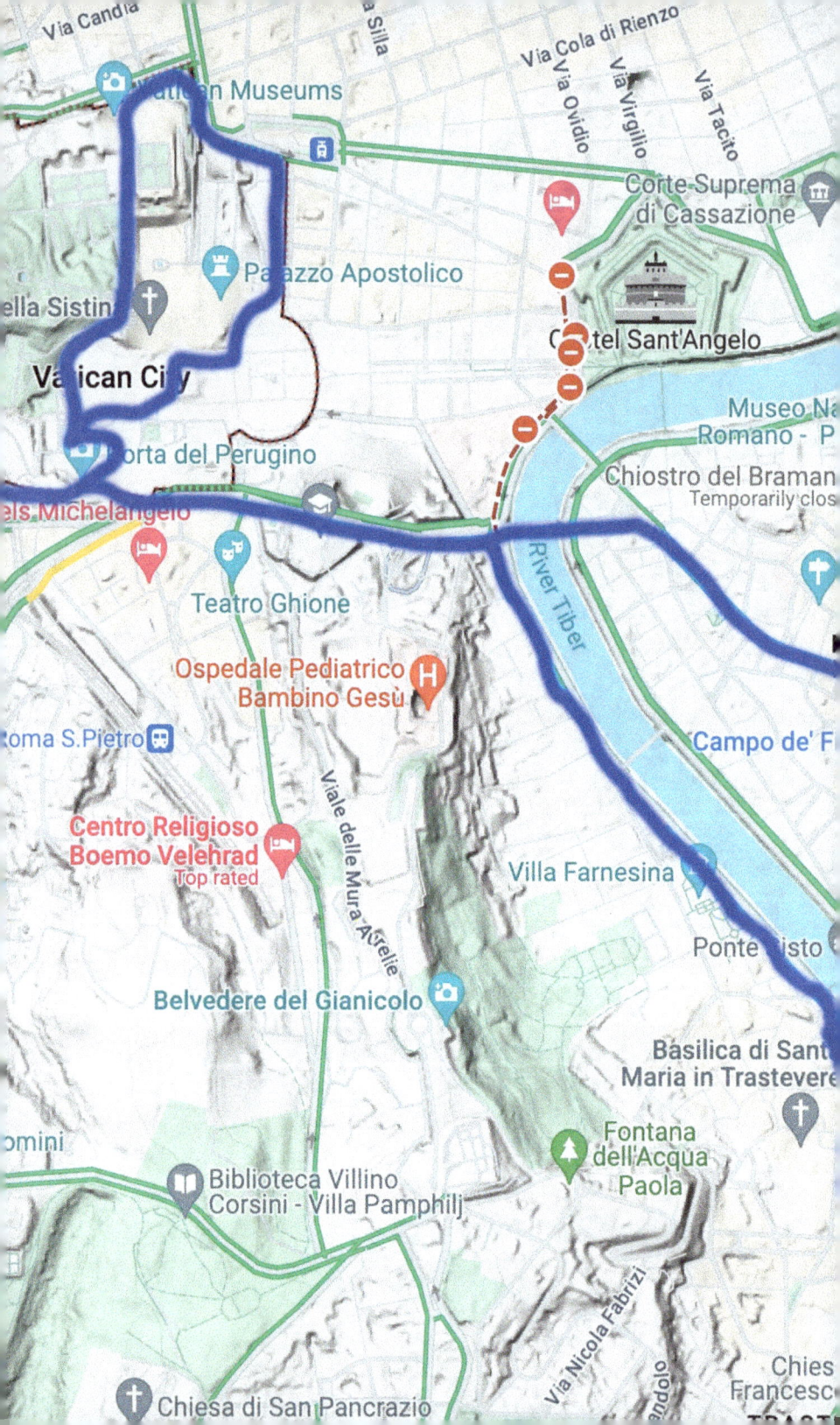

Running Through Rome

STEPHANIE LARKIN

My family has a bit of a reputation for being power travelers. While some people like to spend a week, a month, or even longer in one location to really soak up the atmosphere, we have perfected the art of 'more is more' when it comes to travel. Certainly such high energy travel isn't for everyone, but we've gotten to see the world and get in loads of exercise in the process. Sometimes I think the 1969 romantic comedy "If It's Tuesday, This Must Be Belgium" is a takeoff on our family exploits.

But even for such overachieving and frenetic travelers, our trip to Rome reached new heights. Rome was part of a weeklong trip in Italy, all of Italy, and yes, we even rented an Alfa Romeo to get from one place to another - make that "one city to another" - as quickly as possible. We had one day in Rome, and while you might think that we managed to see nothing, I beg to differ!

I am an over-preparer when it comes to travel, and I read everything possible in advance. I took the Rick Steves 3-day Rome itinerary and decided that we were going to do it all in one day. Yes, we managed, and even squeezed in an afternoon nap to boot.

We had booked an apartment just a block away from Vatican City's western security gate. We arrived in Rome late on a

Tuesday night, and we were up at 7 AM having breakfast in a cafe on that one block walk to Vatican City, and then we waited on line at the security gate. Yes, it was a Wednesday, and our entire Italian trip revolved around us waking up in Rome on a Wednesday so that we could be part of the papal audience.

We made it through the security area, and were ushered by the Gendarmerie Corps of Vatican City into a building, rather than into St Peter's Square. This was not what I was expecting! But the temperatures in Rome were so high that they brought us all into the Pope Paul VI Audience Hall to see Pope Francis. Wow, the Pope and air conditioning - who had it better than us! The enthusiasm in that Hall was electric - more than I could've possibly expected. As visitors from each country were welcomed, a big cheer, and often a song or hymn, thundered through the Hall as each contingent announced its presence. Not knowing what to expect, I felt incredibly underprepared when they announced the United States, and the five of us could do little more that shout our presence and wave frantically, a mere drop in the bucket of the noise generated by previous contingents. It didn't seem to measure up in what was truly an international crowd. Pope Francis finally entered the Hall and the very air in the auditorium changed. We felt both mesmerized and sanctified - seated in air-conditioned comfort rather than standing in sun-drenched, blistering heat. A very good morning indeed!

When our audience with the Pope was over, we all filed out of the Pope Paul VI Hall and our family joined the line of visitors to the Vatican Museum.

I was so glad I had secured timed tickets in advance, as the line for the Vatican Museum stretched around the walls of the Vatican for several blocks. We skipped the line, walked into the Museum, and, of course, followed the map and arrows straight to the Sistine Chapel. You couldn't help but

notice the amazing artwork, and the especially breathtaking ceilings throughout the Museum. Michelangelo is in a class by himself! I was dazzled!

However, If you don't like following rule, then skip the Sistine Chapel. You are not allowed to take out your camera under any circumstances, and they are definitely not kidding. Several tourists were thrown out while we were there; the guards take their jobs very seriously.

After the Sistine Chapel and the other sites and exhibits throughout the Museum, we exited to go to Saint Peter's Basilica. While I have been in enormous churches in my life, nothing quite prepares you for Saint Peter's.

The art, the sheer size, and the feeling that I was on the movie set of "Angels and Demons" overwhelmed me. I didn't quite know where to look first. After taking in such amazing sights as the Pieta and other beautiful works of art throughout Saint Peter's, we exited and returned to our apartment nearby. We were exhausted already, and the heat was getting to all of us, so it was definitely nap time. The Italians have the right idea with siesta!

After a nap, we went out for some lunch and then caught an Uber to take us across to the Colosseum. Boy, am I glad we took that nap! The stairs inside the Colosseum were so steep that each step felt like you were climbing a mountain.

I think the most impressive thing to me about the Colosseum was its floor. Seeing the floor from above, you will see a maze of tunnels and passageways. It looks as if no one could possibly walk on it. However, when the Colosseum was in use, the floor was actually covered by wood so that those visible passageways were below floor level.

Just looking at it from above makes me envision the types of events that were held there, and the different ways they used those passages - those for sport as well as torture. I wonder if they ever imagined thousands of tourists passing through each day, with costumed gladiators outside for photos.

From the Colosseum, we headed next door to the Roman Forum. If I could offer any piece of advice about the Forum, it would be to see it on a cool day. It was hotter than hot when we were there, and it is utterly exposed to the sun. Honestly, I got my best views of the Forum from any vantage point in the shadow of a tree, as I tried to escape from the relentless rays of an unforgiving sun.

We departed the Forum and strolled downhill towards the 'wedding cake,' otherwise known as the Monument to Victor Emmanuel II, and hopped into an Uber headed to the Spanish Steps - all 135 of them! - to begin Rick Steve's Rome - Day 3.

From the Spanish Steps, which lead from the Piazza di Spagna upward to the Piazza Trinita dei Monti, we walked through the heart of Rome, past many other fountains and plazas filled with people, restaurants, and shady characters (urchins who magnanimously hand you roses - and then charge you for them!) The Trevi Fountain - and so many other fountains accenting the streets of Rome - were magnificent, and I loved that there was fresh running water to fill your water bottles at every turn. Goodness, I wish there was one of those up at the Forum!

We had a lovely walk as we explored the sites and shops of picturesque Rome, but rather than settle down for dinner there, we took yet one more Uber to yet another quarter, the Trastevere section of Rome. This beautiful area - on the Vatican side of the river - has a unique Old World charm, with quiet, cobblestone streets and flower-covered alleyways. We stumbled upon a restaurant when we literally paused while walking - and were instantly invited to sit along with another group at the restaurant's (or should that be "ristorante's") outdoor tables. And, in classic Roman fashion, a menu was never actually produced. Instead, heaps of food and wine instantly appeared on our tables - no questions asked, no answers given. Everything was fabulous - if we had been given the opportunity to order, we couldn't have done better! - although the Type-A personality in me always worries when I have no idea what the bill is going to say at the end of the meal. It was a lovely evening, followed by a walk along the river bank and back to our apartment next to Vatican City. All totaled, we clocked over 18 miles of walking, three Ubers, three sit down meals, endless gelato, a Papal audience, three days of Rick Steves itineraries, plus a bonus extra section of Rome even he didn't include. We were exhausted, full, and thrilled to have seen Rome from sunrise to sunset. What a day!

Eternal City, Lasting Memories

STEPHEN DEWOLFE

Rome, Italy, is considered by many to be the "Eternal City," especially by its citizens, who feel that despite rebellions, invasions, earthquakes, and changes in the world, there will always be a Rome.

My one trip to Rome did and does nothing to refute that impression.

I traveled to Rome for business on a Saturday night red-eye flight. After sleeping soundly while flying—a rarity for me—I checked into my hotel, the Bernini Bristol, which was undergoing renovation and surrounded by scaffolding, late Sunday morning and decided to spend the day as a tourist.

I took a taxi to Vatican City and started my trek through St. Peter's Square. The courtyard is actually not a square but is shaped like an ellipse. It is mostly enclosed by a colonnade four Doric columns deep, with a canopy itself topped by more than one hundred statues. I lost count. In the center was an Egyptian obelisk from Roman times and a fountain to each side some distance away. This led to an inner courtyard and the steps to St. Peter's Cathedral itself.

If St. Peter's Square was majestic, the cathedral was glorious.

Side altars that would grace most any church in Christendom, a main altar that makes you know you are in the presence of something greater than any earthly ruler, woodwork and stonework exquisitely worked, dramatic art and sculptures, and a ceiling with a dome that seemed as high as heaven itself. The dome was impressive when seen from the floor of the cathedral, but it was even more so up close after climbing the seemingly endless steps to its rim. Looking outward from openings in the dome, I had a great view of the Square and panoramic views of the city. Looking inward, I could clearly see the inscriptions along the rim, each letter about the size of a person. Looking over the edge, the cathedral floor presented a marvelous and complex mosaic. I wished I had brought a camera; back then, there were no cell phones. I worked my way back to the floor of the cathedral.

It was past mid-afternoon, and I thought I was done for the day as a tourist when I walked past the entrance to the Sistine Chapel. I saw that it was undergoing extensive renovation, and no one was allowed in, but I also noticed the entrance had no gate, guard, or attendant.

I am a law-abiding person, but this was an opportunity not to be missed, so I went in, and my world simply stopped.

The air was redolent with the aromas of unknown solvents, and scaffolding and drop cloths were everywhere. The walls were covered in frescoes. I knew I was in a very special place.

At the time, the Chapel was in the first stages of what would be a ten-year restoration. Some frescoes on the side walls were partially restored, the centuries of accumulated dust, grease, and smoke on one side of the piece and the incredibly bright colors after restoration on the other. This is what the world had been missing for more than four hundred years! The restored parts looked like they had just been painted, and what I had smelled was paint and not solvent. Indeed, I later read about complaints that the colors were so sharp that the restorers must have been "cheating" and applying new paint on the original work.

As intended by the architects and the artists alike, my eyes were drawn heavenward, and the artwork on the ceiling, not yet restored, still took my breath away. I was drawn immediately to Michelangelo's depiction of God and Adam, each extending a hand to the other, and stood with jaw agape. To see it among all the frescoes on the ceiling was nothing like the necessarily small pictures in art books. I admit to staring and waiting for their extended fingers to actually touch when …

My reverie was broken when an unmistakably stern voice behind me shouted a single word in Italian.

Oops, busted!

My father had been a New York Police Department detective, and having learned many things from him, I knew not to move my feet but to open my hands, lift my arms away from my torso, and turn around very slowly. I was facing two uniformed officers, one carrying a machine pistol of some sort (fortunately not pointed at me!) while the other, an older man, had his hand near his sidearm. They were not the ornamental Swiss Guards but instead were either Rome or the national police.

The younger officer expressed his annoyance in Italian, of which I knew little more than "Ciao" and "Arrivederci, Roma." When it was clear that I understood nothing except his unmistakable tone, the older officer motioned me to lower my arms and then spoke in accented English. The message was clear: I should not have entered the Chapel and would have to leave immediately with them as escorts. I nodded and told the officer that I could not resist taking a look inside. To his credit, the older officer smiled and said, "I understand." Happy not to be arrested and glad I had no backpack to be searched or a camera to have the film removed, I retraced my steps out of the Chapel and then around to and through St. Peter's Square without a backward glance.

Whew! Had this episode gone differently, it would have put a crimp in our team's 3-day sales effort with two Italian banks.

After my day exploring in the Vatican, I had no trouble sleeping that night.

With limited time the next two evenings, I climbed the 135

wide-tread Spanish Steps (there were no handrails, but there were three terraces), had a much-needed rest and snack at the top in a nearby café, walked back down (much harder!), and walked then to the Trevi Fountain, with its sculpture and water pools well-lit in the deepening dusk. Yes, I tossed three coins in the fountain.

The next evening, I walked around the outside of the Colosseum, letting the buzzing of vehicle engines and blaring of horns evoke thoughts of crowds at ancient events inside, and peeked inside the Pantheon, its dome larger than that of St. Peter's with an oculus at the top.

I slept well on the return flight on Wednesday and during the subsequent car ride to my home.

A few years later ...

A two-volume, oversized, boxed set was published by Knopf that depicted the art of the Sistine Chapel at pre- and post-restoration stages. It was lauded as the definitive book on the restoration, and after my own experience in the Chapel, I went about acquiring it.

The price was beyond what I could afford. I spoke with Darlene (last name omitted), then proprietress of The Book Corner in Upper Montclair, New Jersey. Our family members were regular customers; our five children could and did walk there and purchase books on account, and I would settle the bill once or twice a month when I was looking and buying for myself.

I proposed an arrangement to Darlene whereby I would purchase the book at $100.00 over her cost, whatever it was. She agreed, and two weeks later, our extensive library received this wonderful addition. It retains its pride of place while evoking great memories and continuous awe of the work of the original artists as well as that of the restoration experts.

Several years later ... The Bernini Bristol Hotel had emerged from its extensive renovations as a five-star hotel.

My eldest son proposed to his girlfriend at the Trevi Fountain and married her soon after.

Today ...

My son and his wife are parents.

St. Peter's Cathedral, the Spanish Steps, the Trevi Fountain, and the Colosseum remain tourist sites.

Rome remains eternal.

And my memories are forever.

An American Schoolboy in the Eternal City

JAMES WEEMS

My first view of Rome was courtesy of the pilot of the Alitalia flight, bringing dozens of tourists into the Eternal City; perhaps having had too much wine, he zig-zagged over the city and dipped each side of the plane to allow us to see the city from above—that, or make use of the air-sickness bags. The beauty of the lights of the city below fought with my fear of heights and flying; I'm still not sure which won.

The group I was with had rooms in a hotel not far from a lot of the major sights of Rome, or at least it seems that way now, remembering it over fifty years later. There were about forty students from my school, plus two teachers. For most of us, this trip was our first time away from family at Christmas. That probably helped the teachers with their chaperoning.

We stayed in Rome for four days. Many of our group used the time to visit the hotel's lobby bar; we had discovered that European customs about drinking alcoholic beverages were much more relaxed than in America, though it was still somewhat unnerving to see a boy barely as tall as the bar itself walk in and purchase a bottle of wine, with no hassles about age or identification—the child handed over the money, the bartender took the money and gave the boy the bottle of wine. I don't even remember a bag being offered or used. I would have missed the exchange, except it occurred as I was sitting at a table in the hotel restaurant near the bar when it happened.

Dinner was always exceptional. Rome and Italy are famous for pasta, and rightfully so, our hotel had a chef who used only freshly made pasta. He scoffed at boxed pasta as "cardboard stuffed inside cardboard boxes." After tasting the spaghetti and sauce he served our first night, I had to agree with him. I believe my classmates must have driven him crazy, though; when he saw them cutting the spaghetti into small pieces, he came running from the kitchen entrance.

"No, no, no! That's ruining the spaghetti!" He was practically in tears. I was trying to use my fork to twirl the spaghetti onto it but kept losing it. He got everyone to watch, and he took my fork and spoon. First, though, he took my table knife, called it an unnecessary beast, and tossed it into the middle of the table. My classmates followed suit, and soon there was a mound of knives. Then he began his demonstration.

"Like this, see?" He slid the fork beneath the edge of the spaghetti with the spoon underneath the fork, then began gently twirling the fork. I moved as if to take over my fork, but he shook his head and finished the twirl. It was an amazing mouth-sized portion of spaghetti, which he dipped into the sauce before bringing it to my lips. I opened my mouth, accepted the bite, and chewed. The entire table erupted in applause, and he bowed.

He headed into the kitchen, returning in a moment to grab all the knives. "You don't need these, do you?" He asked. Everyone answered no, of course.

After dinner, I walked a short distance to the Trevi Fountain. At the time, I remembered a song called "Three Coins in the Fountain," and I just happened to have three pennies in my pocket, so I tossed them into the fountain.

On the second day in Rome, a few of us went sightseeing using a Roman taxicab. All I will say about the taxicab is that it got us to our destination, which was the Colosseum. If you

AN AMERICAN SCHOOLBOY IN THE ETERNAL CITY

haven't seen the real thing, if you've only read about it or been told about it, you haven't really experienced it. Here is a building that stands taller than many of the modern buildings around it and is at least two thousand years old. It looked and felt sturdier than many modern-day constructions.

Of course, there are other remnants of ancient Rome nearby since the seven hills of Rome all feature in the story of the city from its beginning. I vaguely remember Palatine Hill and the Forum, where Julius Caesar met his fate.

Another highlight of Rome was visiting Vatican City, tucked inside Rome. I had seen pictures of St. Peter's on television and in books, but seeing it in person, at least from the outside, was another level of amazing. My group didn't enter the huge basilica because none of us were Catholic, and it wasn't Sunday. Probably not the best reasons, but high-school seniors don't always have the greatest reasoning skills. For me, it was just as impressive seeing the window where the Pope would appear from time to time.

The strangest part of the Rome visit was the side trip to Pompeii, which was still mostly buried under volcanic ash. There was a three-hour-long bus trip to Pompeii, but well worth the ride. How often do you get a chance to see how people lived in ancient times? There are homes and other buildings almost totally preserved like they were just finished being built the day before we arrived. Many of the residents of the town were preserved enough that they could be reconstructed. Seeing the people was a bit weird, though; they looked real enough, but they never moved. Pompeii also featured what high-school-minded kids could only consider a house of ill repute, a brothel. That brought forth a few snickers from several in my group, especially given the bold illustrations on the building.

Returning to Rome after purchasing a few souvenirs in shops around Pompeii and Herculaneum, we passed by Mount Vesuvius, the instrument of Pompeii's doom. Amazingly, there were small towns near the volcano's flank. I wondered if the people living there worried that they might be the next to suffer

Pompeii's fate. It didn't stay in my mind for long because all the walking around Pompeii in the sun had tired me. I soon fell asleep and napped for most of the ride back to Rome. Thank goodness my group roused me when we got to the hotel!

The last day in Rome was bittersweet. For one of the few times in my life, I awoke before any alarm, got myself dressed, and grabbed breakfast in the hotel restaurant. Then I took to the streets of Rome one last time. As I had done each day previously, I had my Kodak Instamatic camera with several extra cartridges of film. I was determined to record as many moments of this trip as possible. There were so many unusual sights to take in, some of which I had seen and overlooked, others I had walked past as I thought about my surroundings. The Spanish Steps, for example, are about a fifteen-minute walk from the Trevi Fountain—I had walked right past the steps in my haste to get to the fountain. I did a lot of walking on my last day; the Piazza Venezia at the foot of Capitoline Hill is less than a mile from the Spanish Steps. The Palazzo Venezia and the monument to Victor Emmanuel II are there, as well as Trajan's Forum, and my camera needed those pictures. Alas, the intervening years have lost all the pictures the camera captured.

With the last day rapidly moving to a close, I reluctantly headed back to the hotel to enjoy a final dinner and prepare for the next day's departure. As I walked through Rome, whether in the presence of the ruins of ancient Rome or just strolling through modern-day Rome, it felt like I faced history at every turn. Of course, I did; Rome is the Eternal City.

Looking for a Great Meal in All the Wrong Places

ADRIAN MILLER

Ah, Rome. Great food everywhere, being devoured in small cafes by people laughing, loving, and drinking copious amounts of wine. Sounds divine, and I was led to believe that I would find such a scene at a little hole-in-the-wall recommended by a friend in NYC. And so, feeling highly enthusiastic and certain we would have one of the best meals of our lifetime, we wandered around some side streets until we happened upon the recommended location. There was not a soul in the place, but undeterred, we assumed that we were just not cool enough to arrive when the hip people came to eat. And so, we stayed, drank a glass or two of wine, and still no one showed up. Feeling slightly confused, we asked the waiter if this was unusual, and he looked at us in contempt and replied, yes. Not at all confident that the food we would order would be edible, we politely paid our bill and wandered a few more blocks until we arrived at a destination where the place was packed with locals; the waiters were welcoming everyone that walked in and embraced us despite the fact that we didn't have a reservation, and optimistic for the second time that evening, ordered what turned out to be the best meal of our trip. Moral of the story, never give up on finding a great meal in Rome.

Roman Holiday
ELAINE GILMARTIN

Rome might not have been built in a day, but it sure as hell can be toured in one. People may say you have kids because you want to relive your own childhood, well, I say we send our kids on study abroad to get a vacay. And so I did.

When my older daughter, Sarah, chose Florence as the destination for her fall semester junior year, it took me about a day and a half to book plane fare for my younger daughter, Katherine, and myself. Did I feel any guilt for not including my husband and my son? Yeah...no. My son had just started college himself and couldn't miss classes, and well, someone had to stay back with the dogs. Sorry, hubby.

With only a five-day itinerary to squeeze in what we could of Italy, Rome was naturally a destination. Shortly before departing, I ran to the local library and found *Rome in a Day*. And so the adventure would begin.

Jet lag is a beast. Neither Katherine nor I slept on the flight to Frankfort, not because some random kid was kicking the back of our seats, which he was, but because neither of us sleeps well on planes, even under the best circumstances. We did, however, begin to doze in the very comfy chairs in the Frankfort Airport during our layover since German engineering also includes furniture, evidently. Hear that, LaGuardia and JFK?!

Anyway, we almost missed our connecting flight to Florence because someone decided to change the gate, and my one semester of college German did not a polyglot make. It was my astute powers of observation that recognized empty seats and a vacant boarding desk is generally not a good sign.

After a quick hop over to Florence, Katherine and I took an Uber to Sarah's apartment and rolled our luggage along the cobblestone street to the ancient-looking doors that were suddenly thrown open. Not having seen my daughter for two months, I hugged her fiercely, eager to see her place and then tour the city. The three of us didn't waste a minute. After determining Katherine to be the bravest to take our luggage up the tiny, rickety elevator, we dropped off our stuff and hit the ground running.

Interestingly, Sarah chose all the inclines for our first day of touring, the four hundred and sixty-three steps to the top of the Duomo and an uphill climb to the Porte Sante Cemetery, all on about twenty minutes of sleep. Despite that, we soldiered on, an espresso midday for a caffeinated boost.

And we saw everything; the David, the Uffizi Gallery, the Cathedral of Santa Maria del Fiore, the Ponte Vecchio. Two full days of walking, cafés, and restaurants with unbelievable food capped off with gelato each night.

We opted to visit Perugia two hours north by train as it coincided wonderfully with the annual Euro-Chocolate Festival. The moment we exited the train, the aroma wafting from the city's center was an intoxicating mixture of Europe's finest chocolates, so rich and decadent we could have floated on it. Of course, when you are walking among tens of thousands of others, it becomes a little more challenging, but tenacity ruled. There was not a piece of chocolate we met that we did not like.

On our feet all day, we got to bed early that night in anticipation of an early start the following morning for Rome. By 7:30, the three of us were seated on the train, coffees in hand. The ninety-minute train ride allowed us to review our relatively short itinerary while watching the Italian countryside whisk by.

For many tourists arriving at the Roman Colosseum by train for the first time, there is a bit of an anachronistic shock. There amidst the traffic and concrete sidewalks, rises in stark contrast a monolith thousands of years old.

"Yup, there it is," Katherine announced.

Crossing the streets with the crowds, we made our way to this iconic piece of history. It was in equal parts impressive and deflating, from the sheer size and architecture to the damage wrought by natural and not-so-natural influences over the centuries.

But my daughters and I were thrilled at what we beheld, and reading about the insanely advanced technology involved, moving floors, retractable ceilings, restrooms, and water fountains at the end of each row, really seemed to put the next thousand years to shame.

From there, we walked the ruins of the Roman Forum and

Palatine Hill until the heat of the mid-October sun led us to seek sustenance and shade.

As we made our way into the heart of Rome in search of food, I would have to say this experience could best be described as running the gauntlet. As we walked along the cobblestone side streets, we were practically accosted by various wait staff trying to entice us to come into their eateries. Exhausted at this point, we found a small, quiet bistro where we were able to rejuvenate our flagging strength.

With renewed vigor, it was on to the Pantheon! I hear that now tourists have to book tickets in advance for a nominal fee, but we were able to save a few euros and simply stroll inside. And those euros came in handy visiting the Trevi Fountain. Not to mention for the gelato.

Now, no trip to Rome is complete without the Sistine Chapel. And it did not disappoint. Struck by its beauty and the chapel's solemnity, we stared upward at Michelangelo's frescoes in awe. The knowledge he went blind from the paint drippings as he lay on scaffolding did not diminish the experience. Truly a timeless masterpiece; it is breathtaking to be in its presence.

Well, our joy apparently did have a time limit.

We knew that with one day, it would be challenging to see everything we wanted, but thought possibly we could try to see St. Peter's Basilica without advance tickets.

Free advice. *Get advance tickets.*

We stood there for a bit, deliberating whether or not we could still make it to our final destination, the Catacombs of St. Callixtus, but standing there behind hundreds of people melting under the October sun, we three became a tad crabby.

My younger daughter plopped down on the ground cross-legged. My older daughter, notorious for her sudden drops in blood sugar, chastised me for not planning better, despite the fact we hit most of the top tourist sites.

Throwing in the towel, we got an Uber to take us out for a scheduled tour at the Catacombs of St. Callixtus, a.k.a San Callisto. With tickets and reservations for the final tour of the day, we arrived in ample time, allowing us to walk around the Appian Way before it began.

As it was now late afternoon, the lowered sun and shade gave us a reprieve from the day's relentless heat. But once the tour guide took our small group of ten or so tourists below ground, I swear it dropped twenty degrees.

Huddling together for warmth, the three of us followed the English-speaking tour guide who shared little-known stories, including how at various points over the centuries, there would be an influx of squatters looking for a place to live. Um, I'd rather take my chances out under the sun, personally.

Its history was tragic, yet also fascinating, and again I was stunned by the engineering prowess two millennia ago. Also thankful there was a way out for us.

Our return train to Florence was 7:30 PM, so we needed to get back. Walking over to the road, Sarah tried to summon an

Uber to retrieve us from the catacombs, but nothing was close. We opted to wait for the passenger bus, which fortunately did not take long.

Well, waiting for it didn't take long, but no one told us about the traffic in Rome.

Creeping inch by inch at some intersections, it felt like Times Square on New Year's Eve. I could feel my blood pressure start to rise as the time ticked by, our train to Florence being the last for the day. I began to imagine having to find a hotel in Rome for our last night in Italy; all of our belongings left at Sarah's apartment, and we in our sweaty clothes. Ugh.

Finally, finally, it pulled up to the stop closest to the trains, and yet, was still a subway ride away. Maybe we were in New York?

Run! I commanded, and we did, down the street, to the subway station, down the stairs, a subway just pulling in at that moment.

And like a good mother, I ran ahead, planning to hold the doors or the train or whatever feat of strength I thought I could muster. Sarah was right behind me and jumped on, and we both turned to see Katherine pushing past a couple of slower people, her backpack falling off her shoulder, and the doors began to slide closed.

Noooo! My panicked mind cried, reaching out for her, and somehow, somehow, she got on just as they closed. Or else I would have had to pull the emergency cord and meet the ire of the Roman commuters. Not that I would have understood the less-than-flattering names I would have been called.

Heart still trip-hammering, we laughed nervously, keenly aware we would have yet another race to the actual train. And so when it pulled to the stop at 7:27 PM, I pushed my daughters ahead this time, the three of us running in lockstep, Katherine muttering something about her backpack, me saying, *just keep going!*

Train after train, we looked desperately at the signs for the destination, Sarah crying out triumphantly when she saw the one for Florence, and we charged ahead, jumping on just as my watch hit 7:31 PM.

With exclamations of relief, we made our way to the first group of seats together, fellow passengers looking up at the trio of laughing, sweaty Americans collapsing into a row of seats.

We made it! I sighed in exultation; no last-minute scrambling to get a hotel room in Rome, no fears of missing our plane back to New York tomorrow, just relief.

As we sat waiting for the train to disembark, Katherine discovered that a half-filled bottle of juice left in her backpack had poured down the back of her leg as she ran to grab the subway, feeling it once she sat.

We laughed at her, as only a good mother and big sister would do, and consoled her by saying had we not run like lunatics, we would have missed the train and maybe even our flight home tomorrow morning.

She conceded that point, resigned to an uncomfortable ninety-minute train ride back to Florence.

And then we sat.

And sat.

And sat some more.

It was nearly 8 PM when the train rolled out of the station.

8 PM.

A difference that would have allowed my blood pressure to remain low, that would have allowed us to saunter to the subway, that would have allowed my daughter a dry train ride back to Florence.

First lesson of Rome is that it is not Zurich. The trains do not run on time.

Ciao, Roma!

ELAINE GILMARTIN

Part 2
And Beyond

The Paradise of a Thousand Roses

BRIAN JONES

Italy is one of the most beautiful countries on this earth. Backpacking across Italy and seeing all the beautiful cities, towns, and majestic regions is really special for any tourist. As you may recall, Rome was one of the most powerful empires. Born here, the Roman Empire—one of the world's most powerful ruling bodies—stretched across Europe, Africa, and the Middle East. As one explores Rome, the history of the buildings, houses, monuments, museums, and churches will astound you. I was always fascinated by Italy's remarkable history, especially the Roman Empire and how it would influence and change humanity as we know it. Strolling through the quaint streets, I remember seeing beautiful houses and romantic couples kissing at the local ristorantes.

Traveling around Italy, one can definitely see how landscapes change as well, but I always love the farms and forests of Italy and the beaches and cliffs overlooking the ocean. Exploring the Vatican and observing the beautiful architecture and the works of famous artists, one can appreciate that Italy is a very old country, aged like the fine red wine served at local ristorantes.

Ever since I was a kid, I have been fascinated with Italy. While there, one can indeed appreciate the food, sunny weather, and the friendly Italians singing, as well as the endless romance in this beautiful nation. I highly recommend anyone who loves good weather and fine food and wants a new adventure to visit Italy. Walking around the Coliseum and the Vatican, one can understand how this small nation influenced the entire world through food, Catholicism, and the Roman Empire. It certainly changed my life. I studied and read countless books on the Roman Empire, emperors, and famous philosophers from Italy, but when one walks around, it's real. It's an engaging experience you will never forget because you are immersed in a foreign culture and deeply enriched by its people who touch your heart. Italy is indeed a paradise of a thousand roses.

Percorso

JOE FARINA

I

roman domes and fountains quicken my blood
masterpieces of travertine marble and engineered water
leave me breathless in its magic and fluid eternity.

night
amplifies the feral sounds
among the alleyways and ruins.
cats stalk,
announcing their kills
with hard growls of pleasure—
they are the true romans here
they come and go at will
among the eternal stones
under their goddess's moon.
they fornicate capriciously
marking the sacred way
for Aradia * with their revelry

splendor, blood and cruel death

fill the coliseum's empty places
the throng that fills its scarred
walkways buzz like drunken flies
a babble of voices rising above
this cauldron of ancient slaughter
redeemed by the wooden cross
anchored to its pitted stones
photographed, a souvenir
of torture, penitent by history
and tourists

II

the tuscan horizon
boasts olive trees and vineyards
manicured in perfect rows
just like the postcards that seduced
us to travel here but without
the thumbtacks holding up
this evening's terra cotta sky.
chiaro scurro furrows and olive orchards
embrace the hillsides
in precise patterns.
Lime white gravel roads
bordered by Mediterranean cypress
cut through the pastoral tapestry
to unseen villas and villages

stone towers stand silently
in the distance, remnants of
medieval fortresses.
I breathe deep the intoxicating belvedere (panorama)
sear its depth and colours into my soul
make love to it in silent song
and poetry, root my feet into its soil

becoming
through it, with it, and in it
under the golden tuscan light

III

Venice
jewel, queen, angel, whore
of the Adriatic.
gondolas, black lacquered
edged in gold, covered against the rain
tethered to striped palinas (poles)
prance in the uneasy surf
with rain and acqua alta (high water)
venice transforms
into a city of umbrellas
clogging tight lanes
pressing in on narrow bridges
the gray light forming a
spectrum of colourful canopies
deflecting the October rain
San Marco-empty-flooding
its perimeter of raised walkways
circled by a babylon of voices and
bright umbrellas

leaves flutter and fall in the ocean wind
salt spray anoints
the paved stones of San Marco's square
tears at our departure

* (Roman cat goddess)

Amalfi Lemons
PATRICIA WALKOW

"Do you need some help, ma'am?" The grocer's question reels me in from a distant shore. "No...no, thank you." *How long have I been standing here? A minute? An hour?*

I stare at the oversized, fragrant lemon cradled in my hand. All around me, sights and sounds seem muffled, as though I'm emerging from anesthesia. I hear shoppers toss apples into brown paper bags, the clunk of D'Anjou pears being placed on a scale, and the thumping of fingers on melons. *Why do people tap melons, anyway?*

A child remarks how fuzzy kiwis are. A young man shakes a head of Romaine lettuce to shed the excess water from the automatic sprayers. Probably no older than thirty, a petite young woman commands her service-vest-clad Yorkie to sit, then heaves a ten-pound bag of Yukon Gold potatoes into her cart. With that thump of spuds against metal, my sight and hearing are restored.

I tune in to the banal music torturing customers. *Did a psychologist write a paper about how insipid music makes consumers buy more onions? Or kale?*

An elderly lady stands beside me at the mounded lemon

display. An old man, his head bowed, his shoulders humped, shuffles next to her. "What are these yellow things?" he asks her in a quivering voice.

"Lemons, Robert. Do you remember lemons?"

He pushes his glasses above his eyebrows and pulls a lemon up to his eyes, then puts it down. He says nothing, then scuffs toward the tangerines, picks one up, peels it, and places it back on the display. I notice the woman has tears in her eyes.

Now fully present, I see I'm in the same store I entered earlier. I'm still standing among the artful arrangement of limes, oranges, and lemons before my mind wandered.

This grocer carries an interesting variety of lemons. The labels tell me they come from Chile, California, Italy, Florida, Spain, India, and other spots across the globe. Some are sallow; others are green-tinged; most are bright, and a few are deep-toned, almost gold-yellow. The majority are oval-shaped, but some are rounded. There are Avon lemons with their wart-like skin and Meyer lemons with their thin, smooth rind. When they are available, the store carries Buddha's Hand lemons, which look like a bee-stung human hand of long, fat, bumpy fingers.

My favorite is the Amalfi lemon from Italy. It's at least twice the size of the average lemon, with a rich, true yellow hue and an intense perfume.

I sometimes think the produce manager at my store has a lemon fetish. But so do I.

I select a few more Amalfis. As I hold their considerable bulk in my hands, I inhale the refreshing bouquet and stroke their textured skin before placing them in my shopping cart. They are beautiful.

These lemons produce mounds of zest, which I will use when cooking fish, chicken, or lemon-mushroom risotto. Their wedges will float in cool water, and delicate, thin, round slices will grace my golden-ginger iced tea with a cheery pop of color, like a dandelion flower. Their air-dried rinds will freshen the air. But before I use them, I will arrange them in a cobalt-blue ceramic bowl on my counter, and they'll reward me with a splash of piercing golden memories...a bright, sunny dress...a banana-colored beach ball floating on a cerulean sea...the Mediterranean.

And Marco.

A few years after college, when I had saved enough money from a job I didn't particularly like, I took a break. No, not a break—I quit. It was the mid-1970s, and that year's spring and summer would be mine to do what I wanted, where I wanted. I figured it would be soon enough when I had to settle into what would become the rest of my life.

I spent a month in Rome, two weeks each in Florence and Venice, a few days at Lago Maggiore and Lago Como, and a long weekend in Milan. I minored in art history in college, and although I had seen many original works of art in U.S. museums, seeing masterpieces *in situ* was breathtaking. After a couple of months, I had grown tired of cities, no matter how magnificent they were.

It was almost summer when I rented a terra-cotta roofed stone villa on a craggy hillside above the Mediterranean, on a curvy stretch of road between Positano and Salerno. To get there, I had to brave driving in Italy. With my heart in my mouth, I managed to escape, unscathed, from Rome in a little red Fiat. *Very* little. Standard transmission. No air conditioning. The Amalfi coast's twists and curls seemed like a glide through still water compared to Rome's tumultuous waves of people and traffic.

My rental was a cottage named *Villa Far Niente*. I couldn't miss its lattice-covered terrace hugging one side of the cottage as I pulled into the short driveway. Deep green leaves woven into the slats offered shade, and lemons hung down like Christmas ornaments. Bush lemons filled large, blue or yellow glazed pots.

Delighted by the yellow-studded view of sky and ocean, I smiled at my well-named vacation house—Villa Carefree.

It was there Marco and I shared wine, cheese, and fruit under a canopy of lemons. In that little house and on that charming terrace of lemon-scented air, I lost myself to Marco in full view of a sparkling-blue lover's sea.

There, too, I came to understand why our romance would never progress yet never recede.

Marco and I met at a gelato stand in Positano. I was enjoying raspberry, and he, chocolate hazelnut. He asked me if I liked mine. I replied in Italian, and he remarked in English that I had beautiful hair.

A flirt. I loved it.

He introduced himself. "I am Marco."

"Susanna," I replied, placing my open palm on my chest.

He politely asked if he could join me on the sea wall, where we sat, looking at the vast expanse of multi-toned blue beyond the bobbing boats. When we finished our gelato, we ambled along the brick path, shared our life stories, and stole glances at each other. He told me he was in the latter part of a three-week vacation from his job as a banker in Milan.

That night, we ate supper together, *alfresco*, by the beach. Before we sat down, he removed the clip holding up my hair. He smoothed my long, dark brown hair with his hands. At dinner, he rolled a small amount of spaghetti on his fork and skewered a piece of calamari. He held it before me, grazed my cheek with his hand, and urged, "Try it."

I did. And swallowed it.

"Do you like it?"

"No," I shook my head.

He laughed at me and poured me another glass of white wine.

I made him try my fish. He leaned his head of thick, dark hair toward me before snatching the fish from my fork.

I peered at his well-formed biceps. His deep-cut shirt, the color of a scarlet hibiscus, plunged lower than my dark brown blouse. His chest bore taut, well-defined muscles, and his tanned skin seemed painted on his body. Sipping my after-dinner cold Limoncello, I wondered: if I tossed a coin at him, would it bounce back at me?

Two nights later, he stayed with me in my bed— overlooking the sea. Our passion insatiable, we awakened at 2:00 p.m., exhausted yet also refreshed. It was a paradox.

He stepped onto the terrace for a moment and returned with the largest lemon I had ever seen. Lounging beside me on the bed, he placed it under my nose. I inhaled its fragrance, and he ran it over my eyes and face, down my neck, and around my breasts. Between my thighs. Every spot the pebbled, leathery fruit touched, he followed with a kiss.

When we finally got out of bed, I understood the sweetness of lemons.

Our affair continued for another seven days of fun, passion, and exploration.

We visited Pompeii, where we watched the restorations in progress and examined vermillion and sunshine-painted murals recently unearthed after centuries under ash. I marveled at the mosaic floors' intricate patterns and representations of people. Up and down the coast, we found seaside restaurants and filled ourselves with gelato, Limoncello, and fish. One day, we rented a small motorboat and headed out to Capri. In full view of a spectacular sunset, we motored away from the island to swim naked in the golden-flamed sea. Whether anyone saw us or not, we didn't care.

One late afternoon in Salerno, under a yellow and white umbrella, Marco leaned across the table while I sipped Campari® and orange juice. He took my hand and brushed it with a soft kiss before holding on to it. "May I ask you a question?"

"Of course. What is it?" I smiled at him.

"Why do you wear such neutral colors all the time?"

I glanced down at my gray linen skirt and white blouse. "I like them."

"Is this something American girls do? Or is it because you are from New York? Every time I see a picture of people there, they are wearing black or gray or brown. Is everyone *in crisi*?"

I laughed aloud and took a sip of my drink. "I don't think everyone's depressed, Marco."

This time, I paid for lunch, though he protested. When we walked away from the restaurant, he clasped my hand. "I want to buy you something. Something bright and playful. Something yellow, like the sun."

"No, you don't have to do that."

"I know...but I'd like to see you in something that matches our mood."

"I don't look good in yellow. It just doesn't work with my skin color."

He stopped, grasped my shoulders, turned me toward him, and examined my face like a dermatologist. "You won't wear the yellow against your face. You will use something navy blue or black or red on your neck first. Come."

"No, Marco. I don't...."

"Come. I insist."

He led me to a shop with a dress form in the doorway. It modeled a crisp corn-colored sleeveless shirt dress with a collar pulled up around its neck. "Look...this is very chic. You should try it on," Marco announced.

"No, please...."

"*Andiamo*, Susanna, *vivi un po*. Live a little," he said. "We are enjoying *la dolce vita*—days of sweetness between you and me. Let's go. *Prego*."

"OK, OK," I nodded in deference. As we entered the shop, the saleswoman smiled and welcomed him in Italian. She told him it was nice to see him again. *Maybe he's brought other girls here.*

Thirty minutes later, I was wearing a small, black silk scarf with diminutive butter-colored polka dots around my neck, and the yellow garment that had been on the dress form was now on my body. It was made of cotton pique with a white floral print and belt; it screamed "vacation." Marco raised the collar to frame my face. He grabbed a coordinating sunhat, arranged it on my head, and smoothed my hair before pulling it back and securing it low on my neck with an ornate white barrette. Then he spun me around to face the full-length mirror. I looked playful, even beautiful, in the outfit. It *had* to be the yellow. It seems I hadn't known how to wear it. The black neckerchief made all the difference.

Or maybe it was the deep blue Mediterranean outside the shop door.

Marco insisted on paying for everything, and as we left the store, I had the unsettling feeling I was a dress-up doll created in an image *he* designed, though I liked what I was wearing. I tucked my discomfort into a pocket of my new dress and didn't think anymore about it.

Our flirtation of food, sex, sun, and water continued for a few more days until the day Marco had to return to Milan. That's when he ruined it.

It was mid-morning, and we had just made love. As we lazed in bed, the white voile curtains billowed in the breeze, sending filtered sunlight across the wooden plank floor and the flaxen plissé bedspread.

Marco stretched his arms and turned toward me. "Make me some coffee," he commanded.

I lifted myself on my right elbow and looked at him as he casually dominated the bed with his head on the pillow and his arms above his head. Turning toward the glass on the nightstand, I took a sip of water, then reached in and picked out a paper-thin round of lemon. I could see light from the windows through it.

Something clicked.

"Coffee? Let's shower and go into town instead." I suggested.

"No, make it for me. That's what a woman does."

Why did he say that? I don't take orders.

Had he said, "How about making us some coffee before I leave?" or "You make the coffee, I'll cut the melon," or "Let's make breakfast together," I would not have recognized the message coming through the translucent lemon slice.

"No, I'm not making coffee," I answered. "This is my place, and I don't feel like using anything in the kitchen today."

He frowned at me.

"And I don't like being ordered around," I added.

"Don't be so sensitive. It's just coffee."

"You assume I'm here to serve you, and that bothers me."

"I don't understand."

"You grab my face and practically force a taste of your meal down my mouth; you buy me clothes I would never buy; you sometimes change my food order at a restaurant, insisting I try what *you* want me to eat. And now, you expect me to get up and make you coffee when I am relaxing after sex, just as you are. It's not about the coffee, Marco. It's about your ordering me to make it for you."

He sighed, got up, and put on his shorts. "I guess I'll head back to Milan now. You can come and visit me if you want, but if you do, there are certain rules. Making coffee for me is one of them." He scribbled his address and phone number on his business card and left it on the nightstand.

Pulling the sheet over my breasts, I sat against my pillow with my knees drawn up to my chest. I watched Marco gather his belongings, knowing I would never be with him again.

"Marco, I can't live the life of a woman as you expect a woman to be."

"That's a pity. We have chemistry."

He was right. We did have chemistry. But it was physical. I was young but wise enough to understand chemistry between lovers needs to be more than physical if the relationship is to last.

Thirty minutes later, he was heading for the door. Donning a gossamer robe, I followed him but did not plead for him to stay. Nor did I apologize. Or cry.

He turned toward me and kissed me goodbye...on the cheek. "*Ciao, bella.*"

"*Ciao*, Marco," I responded, grazing his cheek with my hand.

He started his gray Alpha Romeo, and I watched him turn north on the coast road just beyond the driveway of my little villa. Neither of us waved.

I closed the door and rested my back against it. An hour earlier, we were in the throes of passion. "*Ciao, bello,*" I whispered to him, wondering if he heard me above the whining engine of his sports car as he navigated the snaking Amalfi coast.

Feeling adrift after the intensity of those last minutes with Marco, I pushed myself away from the door. I walked out to the terrace facing the sea as a bantering breeze rustled through the lemon plants and played with tendrils of my hair. I was surprised at my feeling of relief as I plucked a ripe, canary-toned Amalfi from the overhead trellis, caressed its rind, and stroked its smooth leaves. As if in a trance, for hours, I stared at the Mediterranean's depths and followed clouds scudding across the sky. I inhaled the lemon's refreshing aroma, comforted by its ability to encourage clear thinking, and wondered if its acidic juice could provide a kind of primal cleansing. And what of its color?

Lightheartedness and freedom.

Far niente.

Many years have passed since my summer of lemons and Marco—an idyll in *la dolce vita.*

Our brief infatuation was sweet in its moment, though sour in its demise.

But it's mellow in my heart.

It's a lemon wedge steeped in hot, honeyed ginger tea—rich and flavorful, though fully spent.

Yet, it remains bright yellow.

A Day in Venice

DAVID LANGE

September 26, 1997. It wasn't how I imagined it would be. There was no romantic gondola excursion along lamplit canals as a gondolier sang songs of love in Italian while I held the hand of the woman I loved, a bright moon shining in the sky above. There were no kisses upon Renaissance-era bridges. No toasts made with fine Italian wine on the patio of an elegant canal-side restaurant. It was nothing like that—but it was Venice, a place I had always wanted to visit but never had the opportunity to see. I'd make the most of it...and left satisfied and happy.

Aviano Airbase, Italy. Several crews from my home base in England deployed down to this well-established Air Force Base in the north of Italy to support an exercise, and we were having fun flying missions to refuel American fighter aircraft participating in the event. Since the lodging on base was completely booked, we were very "disappointed" to have to accept accommodations in a beautiful hotel in the lovely town of Pordenone. Woe was us. Despite what the Army guys may say about Air Force life, such luxurious lodging experiences were rare. The few times I lucked out were during major events where the usually mandatory military billets were booked and, on account of the off-season, hotel managers were gladly offering rooms at a "government rate" to ensure full occupancy. Of course, no matter how many tents or decrepit old barracks and military lodging facilities I may have stayed at throughout my military career, my sister service brethren would never let me live down the occasional stay in a fancy hotel. It becomes part of the folklore that old soldiers tell their replacements. Truth be told, most soldiers and marines do not, in fact, perpetually sleep under tanks or in foxholes. Interservice rivalry aside, we were pretty thrilled to start our days with a wonderful cup of authentic Italian cappuccino in the glorious lobby of our hotel. But this story isn't about Pordenone or even flying. It does, however, begin with a flying mishap...actually, several mishaps.

Gondola and a boat on a canal

Six recent military flying accidents were six too many. The Chief of Staff of the U.S. Air Force directed all units to stand down for a "Safety Day." We knew what this meant—our time in the air would be exchanged for extensive and exhausting safety briefings, which would surely rehash, yet again, the stories and lessons we had frequently heard before. We did our best to stay engaged throughout the training, but there wasn't one of us who wasn't watching the clock during our two-hour safety briefing and discussions. We all had things we wanted to do and places we wanted to go on this unexpected, yet very welcome, day off. I had already begun to canvas the group to see if anyone might be interested in heading to Venice with me. I wasn't sure there'd be another opportunity. Most of the guys just wanted to hang out locally and find some nice "watering holes" to partake of various alcoholic beverages while they engaged in some "people watching" from one of the lovely sidewalk cafes. I loved the cafes, too. Especially in the nighttime, there was something magical about sitting out there, watching masses of interesting characters pass by while enjoying some tasty Italian food and a drink of your choice. One of my favorite memories is hearing the church bells ring across the city. The bells added a certain charm to the scene that filled my heart. For all that, when faced with the option, I typically chose to explore historical sites and cultural immersion over just drinking and talking. I was happy to combine the two, but experience had informed me that I would, in all likelihood, have to sacrifice Part B of my plan as a lovely outing at a sidewalk café (Part A) turned into an evening of "bar hopping." That wasn't going to happen this time—not with a real shot at finally seeing Venice weighing in the balance.

I finally managed to find another person interested in seeing Venice—one of our enlisted Boom Operators. Boom Operators are a fun bunch, men and women who maneuver the refueling boom in the back of our aircraft to actually make the contacts with receiver aircraft so that we can transfer fuel. The Technical Sergeant and I agreed that we'd head for the train station as soon as our Safety Day activities were done. As specific military protocols are involved, especially between officers and enlisted members, we elected to go with a little more informal use of our crew positions (always used in the jet) for our excursion rather than calling each other Captain and Sergeant all day long. Thus, "Nav" and "Boom" headed off on our adventure.

Needing money for the trip, we first stopped at an ATM so

my travel companion could get some Italian lira. And that's when the machine "ate" his card. This was not good. We were on the clock as my comrade tried to connect internationally with his bank to find out what was going on. Apparently, since he hadn't used that specific account in a very long time, his account was locked. Thus, the card was de-authorized, and the ATM machine was digitally instructed to keep the card. This was all very odd... and frustrating...for both of us. When it seemed that progress was unlikely, I assessed the funds I had exchanged into Italian lira and concluded that I could cover the cash expenses for both of us if we were careful about expenditures. With financial matters settled, we headed for the train station and began our hour-and-a-half journey from Pordenone to Venice. We rode on the top of a double-decker train, and I enjoyed the scenery between passages from the Venice guidebook I had purchased. I knew time would be of the essence once we arrived, so I carefully planned a touring route between the key sites I wanted to see while noting the operating hours, where applicable.

Once our train pulled in, we were off to the races. Well, I was off to the races. Shortly into our tour plan, I discovered that my traveling partner had bad knees, and the aggressive pace I was setting was not going to be sustainable. With my camera at the ready, we agreed to do our best, stopping where needed and adjusting our pace to make the experience enjoyable for the two of us.

A DAY IN VENICE

Gondolas on a Venetian canal

After snapping several gondola photos and scenic shots down a few canals, we made our way toward objective number one, or "numero uno," as they say in Italian. This was, of course, the famous St. Mark's Square (Piazza San Marco) and the great church (Basilica di San Marco), along with the famous St. Mark's Campanile, the spectacular 323-foot bell tower of St. Mark's. St. Mark's is the heart of Venice, and I was spellbound by its grandeur.

St. Mark's Basilica

The famous Piazza did not disappoint—pigeons blanketed the square just as I had seen in numerous movies. Our first tourist stop was the absolutely stunning Basilica San Marco. Entering this giant edifice leaves the visitor filled with awe. The Basilica is a remarkable blending of Eastern and Western influences, representing a cultural accumulation grown over six centuries. Adorned with marble and gold and filled with breathtaking mosaics, carvings, and statues, few locations are as opulently magnificent as this. Besides the church itself, there's also an attached museum, a treasury, and various chapels. The museum houses, among other things, the original "Triumphal Quadriga," four bronze horses stolen from the Hippodrome in Constantinople in 1204 whose origins are believed to date back even much further than that. The horses were originally placed outside the Basilica, upon the facade, but were looted by Napoleon in 1797. Returned in 1815, the original bronze horses eventually found their way to the safety of the museum in the 1980s to help preserve these remarkable works of art. Replicas replaced the originals on the Basilica's exterior.

Following a rather extensive visit to the Basilica, we headed for the Campanile, the impressive bell tower that reaches skyward from St. Mark's. The wait to get to the top was well worth it. From atop St. Mark's Campanile, you are treated to a magnificent view as Venice spans out before you. You can see the intricacies of the city and, on a clear day, you can even see the distant peaks of the Alps. From our spectacular perch, high atop St. Mark's Piazza, it was easy to lose track of time. With the day waning, we decided we had best get moving lest we miss an opportunity to spend some time at the famous Doge's Palace, or Palazzo Ducale.

St. Mark's Campanile

The Doge's Palace began its life in the 9th century as a fortified castle to protect the elected chief magistrate of Venice, the doge, and members of the government. Unlike our politicians, the Doge was elected for life from within the aristocracy of Venice. Venice became a very wealthy city due to its unrivaled international trading practices. It should come as no surprise, then, that the Doge's Palace is a tour de force of decadent opulence. Like many structures in Venice, the original was lost due to fire, but the current palace was rebuilt in the 14th and 15th centuries. The Gothic architecture is stunningly beautiful. The interior is, likewise, a masterpiece of craftsmanship reminiscent of Versailles, with grand halls and elaborate carvings across its four floors. Unfortunately, there was little to no furniture on display, but this did not detract from the splendor of the palace. On the exterior, we made sure to see the beautiful "Bridge of Sighs," an enclosed white limestone bridge that connects the interrogation room in the Doge's Palace with the prison across the Rio di Palazzo. Many prisoners got their last look at Venice, and freedom, through the windows of this bridge.

The last museum we tried to visit was the Naval Historical Museum but, unfortunately, the sands had run out on our hourglass, and we reached the museum after its closing time. For all that, I would not have traded a minute in the Doge's Palace for a chance to slip in, with minutes to spare, to the Naval Museum. With no more time-critical events on our schedule, we navigated some of the small backstreets of Venice to explore the city. Then, we made our way back to the Grand Canal, where we enjoyed a leisurely stroll along the banks, including a trip across the exquisite Rialto Bridge. After a day of racing about, we definitely enjoyed the slowdown. My travel companion's knees had taken about all the pounding they could stand, and there wasn't a lot of mileage left in them.

A DAY IN VENICE

Gondolas along the Grand Canal

With the sun dipping below the horizon, we found a wonderful little restaurant alongside the Grand Canal where we could dine while watching the traffic along the waterway. I kept it simple and ordered a delicious plate of spaghetti. At dinner, especially, I missed not having my wife with me, and I'm sure my travel companion was feeling the same. For all that, we made a really fun day of it and had great conversations on the late-night train ride back to Pordenone about our fantastic adventures in Venice. No, my first trip to Venice wasn't as I imagined it would be, but the city itself absolutely did not disappoint. There were so many things I wanted to see and not nearly enough time to see them all...but I saw what I most needed to see—the magic of one of the world's most enchanting cities. I eagerly await the day when I can return once more and perhaps share the experience with someone special.

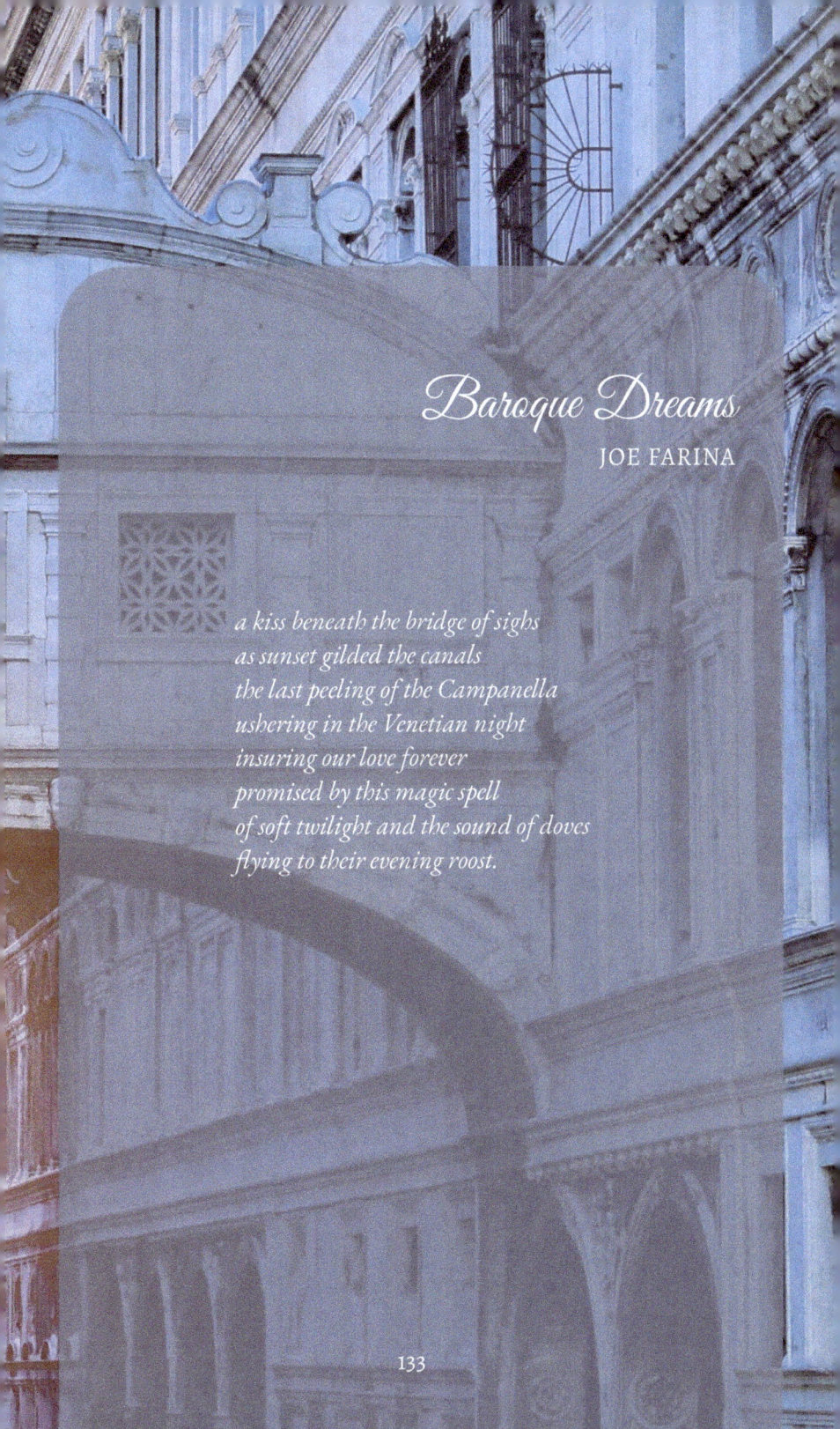

Baroque Dreams

JOE FARINA

a kiss beneath the bridge of sighs
as sunset gilded the canals
the last peeling of the Campanella
ushering in the Venetian night
insuring our love forever
promised by this magic spell
of soft twilight and the sound of doves
flying to their evening roost.

All Venice is a Falling...

JOSEPH A FARINA

Title by Amy Lowell

city of vacant piazzas
and deserted terraces
conquered by pools of rain
and acqua alta washing over
canal embankments
it's cold waters seeping
under Byzantine doors
cascading down marble stairways
inundating ancient crypts, over
mosaic epitaphs of princes
and doges tombs, the mad dance
of swirling water riding rising
ignoring the gilded pavilions and
carved balustrades of the jewel city
lacquered icons flake to wet fingers
rippling in the minor currents of
the silent sanctuary underground

STEPHANIE LARKIN

Venice shuddering in its slow collapse
her light extinguishing upon the world
her Devine protection slowly eroded
by the blossoming winds and tide
no longer their master

Karen (aka Grandma) and Rachel's Italian Adventure

NOVEMBER 2018
KAREN SHAW AND RACHEL ABRAHAM

How much do you love your children? No less than 100% each child, I'm sure. And then a grandchild comes into your life and turns everything topsy-turvy. That love is beyond anything you have ever imagined. So when they face disappointment of any kind, you want to do something—you will do anything for them. Having said that, what did I do when I saw disappointment on my granddaughter's face? I started thinking, "How can I help her? What can I do to put a smile back on her face?" Then it came to me.

My granddaughter Rachel planned to take a mini vacation with some friends—an extremely special one that doesn't come along too often—but her trip was canceled. I, too, had planned a trip. Mine was to visit friends in Japan, but as these things often happen, it, too, was canceled. So there we were, sitting at my dining room table commiserating when suddenly the lightbulb over my head lit up, and without thinking, I just said, "So let's go somewhere." And she replied equally as fast, "Are you serious?!?" I laughed and said, "I guess so!" And that's how our adventure began. And that's how a lifelong dream of mine became a reality. I always wanted to be able to take her on a trip, and now we're actually going! Out came that smile—on both of our faces, I might add.

It didn't take us long to decide on Italy—beautiful, romantic, Tuscany—Florence, to be exact, and the planning began. The more we planned, the more real it became. And the more exciting!

Major concentration and organization came next... How to get there? Where to stay? Where to eat? What to do?

Days of sorting out different flights—days, times, (prices). Which is good for you? What's good for me? Finally, done! I was working that day near Penn Station in NYC, so our adventure actually began on a train to the airport. Our flight included stopping in Munich for an hour, then on to Florence, where we had reserved a car to take us from the airport to the hotel. Neither of us spoke in the car as we just sat, devouring the scenery—the Tuscany countryside and those beautiful Cypress trees that appear everywhere. Then there we were—in the center of Florence. We were in Italy! Better yet, Tuscany! I mean, who hasn't seen *Under the Tuscan Sun* or *Letters to Juliet*?

Now for the hotel. Neither of us had the slightest idea as to precisely where, the type of room, amenities, location regarding restaurants, shops, transportation, etc. (and did I mention price?) So, as with the flights, by the process of elimination, we finally selected a hotel—the Hotel Laurus al Duomo right in the heart of the beautiful city of Florence. The hotel was charming, the room lovely with a magnificent view, and the concierge friendly and helpful.

Hotel Laurus al Duomo

The day we arrived, we decided to just walk around the city and explore, taking lots of photos, of course. Rachel's fascination was held by the tiny cars we saw parked along the streets in the most beautiful colors. Our hotel was down the road from the Duomo/Basilica and its surrounding buildings, and we passed them by almost every day. They are off-white with their edges outlined in dark grey—the same color as the lead in a Number 2 pencil. I referred to these buildings as the pencil drawing buildings (photo on opening page)—not to be disrespectful, but that's what they resembled to me.

I was fascinated by their architecture as well as their coloring. We walked some more, taking in the city's artists' street art, and selected an interesting-looking restaurant, enjoying a delicious dinner as we ate outdoors. We also found a fabulous place to buy our gelato that first night. After all, what's more important than gelato in Italy? Rachel tried different flavors each time while I enjoyed my favorites—chocolate and coffee. Deliziosa!! So good; it was the only place to go as far as we were concerned. Then we walked farther down, ending up in a square where a beautiful, working carousel stood, all lit up, going round and round, while street singers entertained us as we sat around, listening and eating our gelato.

Our Gelato (top)
In the square (bottom)
Street singers with carousel (bottom)

We had breakfast at the hotel every morning on a terrace overlooking the city—the view was spectacular, and the food was so fresh and tasty. Neither of us had ever tried blood orange juice before. We loved it and looked forward to having it every morning with our breakfast. So first came the juice, then the heavenly eggs and toast, and, of course, a little cake for dessert with espresso. And so began our days.

This is now a reality! So exciting!

Next... What will we do there other than eat and shop? We need to book a few tours before the trip and find out about some restaurants. I discussed this with a few friends and was now armed with the names of several of "the best restaurants in all of Florence," especially those in out-of-the-way places. And this is where a Facebook group, "The Tri-State Restaurant Club," came in handy. It seems they are well-versed in restaurants here and abroad, not just in New York, New Jersey, and Connecticut. I asked if anyone could recommend a restaurant in the Florence area and was overwhelmed by the number of places they shared.

La Giostra (top)
Ristorante Buca Dell'Orafo (bottom)

We probably could have stayed six months and eaten each meal in a different restaurant—that's how many we received. We took the one with the most recommendations —La Giostra (photo right)—way off the beaten path, where tourists aren't found. It had a magnificent ceiling that was built in the 1500s, the ambiance was amazing, the service spectacular, and the food exquisite! Another restaurant had been recommended to us by a friend, Ristorante Buca Dell Orafo (photo right). She said it was also off the beaten path—no tourists there. You walked downstairs into the restaurant, and did we luck out! There was only one table available in the entire (small) restaurant; thankfully, it was for two. The menu was in Italian, our waitress didn't speak English, and it was her first day on the job, to boot! Fortunately, the couple sitting next to us noticed our dilemma and was nice enough to translate both the menu and the waitress. The food was way beyond deliziosa, and all went well. The rest of the time, we just walked into a restaurant that looked interesting—even one that served zucchini/cheese pizza. OMG—more delicious than we had imagined. Not one restaurant, large or small, was even the slightest disappointment. Each one had its own charm and amazing food. (photos below)

Pizza for lunch at Ristorante La Grotta Guelfa

So, check! Another unknown taken care of. Next came the tours.

We decided to pre-plan three day tours. The first one we came up with was a sunset trip to a winery in Siena, also in Tuscany, for dinner and wine tasting—The Sunset Siena and Chianti Wine Tour with Dinner. How romantic is that? Our tour bus arrived in Siena early, and the story of the City of Siena and its fascinating horse race in the town square unfolded. We learned about the famous Palio di Siena (Race of Siena)—ten horses with their riders sitting bareback, racing twice

The Siena Horserace (top)
Siena Square, seen from where we sat (bottom)

a year, every July 2nd and August 16th—as thousands gather in the square to cheer them on. And there we were, sitting in that very square (photos on previous page) with espresso (for me) and gelato for us both (of course), as the sun set. Could it get much better than this? We highly doubted it.

After about an hour, we met with our group and the tour guide, boarded the bus, and were on our way to the winery, where we were given a tour, then a three-course meal, paired, of course, with the correct wine.

The next day, we decided to take a walk on our own and visited the Great Synagogue of Florence, the most beautiful synagogue I had ever seen. The exterior architecture of the building, as well as the landscaping, were stunning, with the inside even more so. (photo right) The workmanship on the wooden pews is magnificent, the grand tiles on the walls and ceiling, and the lighting and shapes of the doorways and ceilings are breathtaking. (photo below) We signed the guest book and left our mark.

Rachel in front of the synagogue

The interior of the synagogue

Next, we reserved a bus and train tour to Rachel's favorite—Cinque Terre, five fabulous towns—and at 7:00 am, we were on our way. Unfortunately, we could only visit three out of the five as there were terrible rains just before our arrival in Florence. One of the towns suffered mudslides, and the other flooded out; therefore, each was closed to all travelers.

Cinque Terre
Our romantic guitar player, the view from our restaurant, and spectacular colors

I think it was the second town we visited that I enjoyed the most, where the heavenly Spaghetti alle Vongole was the best I have ever eaten, along with a little vino and espresso for dessert. Rachel also loved her scrumptious ravioli and her dessert—gelato, of course. To complete the picture, we noticed a gentleman sitting a short distance away from us with a guitar on his lap. (photo above) Suddenly, he began to sing, serenading us as we ate our pasta, looking over at the dazzling water ahead of us. (photo above)

Each town had its own personality, with colored houses along the mountainside, gorgeous inlets in front of where the boats moored (photo above), cobblestone walkways, and fabulous shops. We loved each and every one of them. (photo right) As an aside, we learned why the homes were painted in different colors. It was so that the men, coming off their fishing boats after hours of working at their strenuous jobs, would know which

Rachel and Karen at Cinque Terre

house was theirs. Evidently, years ago, some entered the wrong house when they returned in the middle of the night, too exhausted to check carefully. (Interesting, isn't it?)

The third planned excursion was to the magnificent Tuscany countryside, where we spent hours learning how to make pizza and gelato, our new favorite food.

After disembarking from our tour bus, we enjoyed appetizers and wine on the patio with the rest of our group, overlooking the olive trees, lemon trees, and various vegetables and fruits planted there. (Photo right) We then went inside to begin the process of preparation for the gelato. We donned our aprons and proceeded to follow the instructor's call. Rachel was our hands-on chef, and I was her sous chef. We all selected our flavors—Rachel and I chose mint. Each team had all the tools we needed to create the gelato from scratch. Rachel used a mortar and pestle to grind down the fresh mint (photo below), a scale to weigh the milk and cream, a mixer and a bowl to combine all the ingredients, measuring spoons for the sugar, a spatula, and a container to place in the freezer for the gelato once it was prepared. (Photo below)

Overlooking their garden

Gelato lessons
Rachel with mortar and pestle, crushing the mint (Left)
Gelato tools (Right)

While it was freezing and becoming gelato, we went outside to the brick oven area on the patio and began learning how to make the best personal pizza ever with a lovely glass of wine. (Photo right) We sat at a long table lined with various toppings all along the center, with flour and yeast at each place. We learned how to spin the dough, throw it in the air, and then catch it. Rachel did that well—I was too chicken even to try, but I did make my own dough—something new to add to my repertoire. The toppings included basil, tomatoes, onions, artichokes, mushrooms, several meats, and various other veggies, all fresh from their garden, as well as sauce and cheeses. (Photo right) With the dough ready, it was time to spread the sauce and cheese, then select and place whichever toppings we

Pizza lessons
Brick oven (Top)
Pizza toppings (Bottom)

wanted onto our pie. We even learned the correct way to put the sauce on the dough—who knew? There's a method for everything...

We returned to check on the gelato once the pizza was in the brick oven. It was then that our instructor showed us how to use liquid nitrogen. (Photo right) He made gelato in seconds with not only the normal flavoring but also flash-froze edible flowers along with sage and created the most delicious gelato in only minutes! We passed the bowl around, and each of us enjoyed a taste. (Photo right)

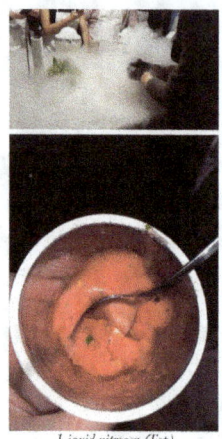

Liquid nitrogen (Top)
Delicious end result (Bottom)

So, now that the pizza and gelato were ready, we each went to the oven and took our pizza, bringing it inside, where there were long picnic tables for us all to eat and get to know each other. (Photo below) There were husbands and wives, boyfriends with their girlfriends, boyfriends with their boyfriends, parents, and (older) children. I believe we were the only grandmother/granddaughter duo in the group. Of course, we all loved ours—what could be bad? Next, we went to a long table where each gelato flavor was in a bowl along with different toppings, red salt among them. This was wonderful as we could taste all the different flavors everyone had made. (Photo below) We then went outside again and each of us received a diploma! (Photo below) The entire experience was amazing, to say the least.

KAREN (AKA GRANDMA) AND RACHEL'S ITALIAN ADVENTURE

Rachel's pizza just out of the oven, Gelato in several flavors/toppings, Receiving our diplomas,

Back in Florence, we tried but weren't able to view the original David. We were somewhat disappointed, but enjoyed our walk through the square where various artists sat and told stories. (Photo right) We had already learned an interesting tidbit on one of the tour buses. The story tells of Michelangelo being forced to use an inferior marble slab to sculpt the statue of David, as it was the only one large enough in the entire area. Interesting, yes? We were sorry to have missed it but were unaware that the line would be so terribly long. Having already made other plans, we could not wait. Since there were several copies sporadically placed in various areas of Florence, we did get to see him eventually.

Square in Florence with artists

We spent a great deal of time shopping at the Ponte Vecchio Bridge, famous for its shops (mostly jewelry) that line the sides and are open to pedestrians only. (Photo right) Of course, we did most of our spending at the small kiosks with vendors selling everything—scarves, gloves, all kinds of leather goods. There were three major areas of kiosks. They lined both sides of the path in one area, and all together in a group in another, which sold mostly leather garments, wallets, etc. Then there was a third area where they sold mostly t-shirts, hoodies, and sweatshirts.

We shopped everywhere for everyone back home, purchasing a few things for ourselves, as well. Towards the end of our trip, I suggested we split up and shop for each other—just a small gift for each of us to remember this wonderful adventure. We planned to meet up in an hour, which we did. Later, back in our room, we gave each other our gifts. Such a great idea and so much fun.

Karen
On the Ponte Vecchio Bridge

Later that day, just prior to sunset, we took a taxi to the Piazzale Michelangelo which is high up, overlooking the city, just to watch as the sun set over Florence and the River Arno. (Photo right) It was the most magnificent sight, with the multi-colored sky and the city's lights coming on, creating a piece of art any museum would be proud to own. There was also one of the David statues up there, lit so beautifully. (Photo previous page) We stayed a while, taking photos, of course, and then we decided to leave. We assumed there would be no problem getting a taxi to take us back, since this was a big

Piazzale Michelangelo
Rachel and Karen (Top)
Statue of David (Bottom)

touristy place, but were we ever wrong! Not a cab in sight, and I had no phone service up there. I overheard two young men reserving a car and asked if we could do the same, but it was suggested we share the ride with them. We did and had such fun! One was from New York, visiting his friend who was studying in Florence, and the other was that friend, and he was from Boston. Our conversation suddenly became all about the New York Yankees vs. the Boston Red Sox. Thank goodness it was a short ride as my sports knowledge leaves a lot to be desired, and we had just enough time to deplete it without anyone suspecting.

We walked around after that, and that's when it happened. I fell off the curb. Nothing terrible, but my arm was all scraped and bleeding. We went to a farmacia, where they proceeded to act as an emergency room. They washed it, put some medicated ointment on it, and then bandaged it up. I have to say, we were pleasantly surprised at this treatment.

We then went for gelato. I think it was to put a smile on my face, serving as the lollipop reward you would get for being a good girl in the doctor's office. And it did its job.

Train Station (Top)
The Leaning Tower
from our photo book (Bottom)

Another trip that wasn't a previously reserved tour, was to see the Leaning Tower of Pisa. We walked to the train station, bought our tickets, and boarded the train for an hour's ride to Pisa. (Photo right) We found the Tower after walking in the wrong direction, but, thankfully, not for too long. This was something I had learned about as a child—something so famous that everyone knows it. And there it was—an awesome sight to behold right there in front of us. (Photo on previous page). We saw many older people going all the way up to the top, so I bought tickets. We walked into the Tower, and that's when I uttered these now-famous words: "Where's the elevator?" Of course, as they were being said, I realized what I was saying, and the two of us just laughed. Needless to say, we did not go up to the top, but those three words made it into our photo book and still make us laugh each time we see them.

So now we've come to the end of our adventure. The car was coming to the hotel to take us to the airport at 11:00 am. Therefore, we ran out of the hotel at 10:00 am to get our last taste of that wonderful Italian gelato. (Photo right) And while we were there, we decided to check out a kiosk or two as you can never shop too much while on vacation. We walked to where the vendors were and found only florists—loads and loads of beautiful flowers with colors and aromas that just made you smile. (Photo right) Then there was a parade! Were they seeing us off or were they happy we were leaving? Neither, actually, although we never did find out what it was for. It was pretty, though, and lively with lots of music. So we decided to consider it as a sendoff from Florence to us. (Photo next)

Our last day, 10:00 AM
Enjoying our last gelato (Top)
And all those flowers (Bottom)

Our flight home took us to Zurich for about an hour to change planes, and we walked around their beautiful airport.

The Swiss airline fed us pizza

and chocolate—not too nutritious—but good, healthy nutrition is at home, so we just couldn't turn it down.

Now we're back home in New York, exhausted and about five pounds heavier. Rachel is in a cab to Brooklyn, and I in one to Bayside.

How lucky are we to have had this experience with each other? It's not often we get to live out a dream.

The adventure is over, but we will remember this all our lives. We each have a photo book that encompasses our special memory, as it brings tears to our eyes and puts smiles on our lips, all at the same time. I guess I did it!

I have seven grandchildren in total, so the mystery now is where and with whom the next adventure will be, and I can't wait to live out another dream. How lucky am I?

So here's to Rachel and Tuscany. CinCin and Ciao! You know what? I love you...

A parade on our last day

Ciao Florence!

Our beautiful Italian adventure, remembered...

Proposal Upon the Rialto

JOE FARINA

history marks this place
by princes, popes and lovers
water reflecting moon and stars
liaisons and secret trysts
water carrying venetian naves
commerce to the world
crossed by this bridge that
knows the secret desires of kings
plotting war and scoundrels
planning their evening seductions

beyond, the blessed st marks spires
look down upon each bridge of sighs and joy
and this - the heart -
gold and silver merchants entice tourists
but i see only the sicilian eyes
of a dark haired girl more brilliant
than the diamond that offers her my pledge,
here, upon rialto bridge.

Meet Our Contributors

Donna Keel Armer is the author of Solo in Salento: A Memoir which has been translated into Italian as Un'americana in Salento. She recently completed a book tour of Southern Italy. Her newly released first novel The Red Starfish is Book #1 in the Cat Gabbiano Mystery Series. She's a photojournalist who has published articles in magazines and anthologies on travel, food and wine, home and garden and various other topics. She lives with her husband in the South Carolina Lowcountry where she's a docent at the Pat Conroy Literary Center, a member of SAGE and the Sea Island Spirit Writers.

Vanessa Caraveo is an award-winning bilingual author, published poet, and artist who has a passion for promoting inclusion, empowerment and equality for all, helping others discover the power they possess within themselves to overcome adversity and persevere in life. She is involved with various organizations that assist children and adults with disabilities and enjoys working with non-profit groups and volunteering in the promotion of literacy. Vanessa aspires to continue making a positive difference in many lives through her service to others and literary work.

C. D'Angelo is the award-winning Women's Fiction author of The Difference and The Visitor, whose novels consist of relatable stories of the Italian American culture, bursting with food, tradition, history, travel, and quirky characters. When not writing, she can be found at home in Florida enjoying time with her husband, playing ukulele, drawing, crocheting, and partaking in a variety of other artistic endeavors.

Find out details about C. D'Angelo's books, get freebies from her newsletter, and more at: www.CDAngeloAuthor.com

---

Steve deWolfe is an IT professional by vocation and a poet and writer by avocation. His unique point of view has brought life to such subjects as a baseball in flight and a video camera on Christmas Eve. His poetic tributes to championship high school cross-country and girls' softball teams were presented at season-ending celebrations. He has composed poetry for birthdays, anniversaries, and weddings for family and friends. His "Final Flight - a baseball's story" was published in baseballbard.com and was accepted by the National Baseball Hall of Fame. His poetry has been published in five Red Penguin anthologies, and his travel writings have appeared in Red Penguin's collections for London, Paris, and now, Rome. Steve was born and raised in Brooklyn, NY, lived in New Jersey for nearly 50 years, and is currently enjoying the weather, writing and work in Jacksonville, Florida. steve.dewolfe@gmail.com

MEET OUR CONTRIBUTORS

Linda Trott Dickman is an award winning poet, author of four chapbooks and a poetry prompt book for children of all ages. Her work has been anthologized locally and internationally. She is the coordinator of poetry for the Northport Arts Coalition. Linda works with poets of all ages, at the Walt Whitman Birthplace Association, local museums, and leads a poetry workshop at Samantha's Li'l Bit O' Heaven coffee house.

Linda is a New York State Woman of Distinction for the year 2023. She makes a linguine and clam sauce recipe that is as old as she is. She loves singing in her church choir. She is a punster.

Joseph A Farina is a retired lawyer in Sarnia, Ontario, Canada. An award winning, push cart nominated, internatianally published poet , his works published in many poetry magazines notably Quills Canadian Poetry Magazine, The Windsor Review, and appears in the anthologies *Sweet Lemons: Writings with a Sicilian Accent, Canadian Italians at Table, Witness and Tamaracks: Canadian Poetry for the 21st Century*. He has had two books of poetry published—*The Cancer Chronicles* and *The Ghosts of Water Street* and an E-book *Sunsets in Black and White* and his latest book, *The beach, the street and everything in between*.

Elaine Gilmartin is a therapist by profession, which is a great career for writers because she get into people's heads and hear stories that can seem too fantastic even for fiction. It's also helpful in that it is her job to challenge how they perceive themselves and the world around them, not always an easy task! Travel is Elaine's passion, especially if she can find a local marathon. Elaine write articles for the online site Medium and loves to start each day with a long run.

MEET OUR CONTRIBUTORS

Mark Andrew Heathcote is an adult learning difficulties support worker. He has poems published in journals, magazines, and anthologies online and in print. He resides in the UK and is from Manchester. Mark is the author of "In Perpetuity" and "Back on Earth," two books of poems published by Creative Talents Unleashed.

David Lange was born and grew up on Long Island, New York. A graduate of the United States Air Force Academy, he served for 30 years as an Active Duty officer in the United States Air Force before retiring in 2018. Colonel Lange is a decorated combat veteran and flew numerous combat, combat support, and humanitarian relief missions during his career. He was awarded the prestigious Institute of Navigation Superior Achievement Award in recognition of his life-long accomplishments as a practicing navigator. David loves sharing stories of hope and inspiration. He has numerous short stories, essays, and poems published within various anthologies and his memoir, "Quest: My Journey Through La Mancha," was published in 2020.

Rex McGregor is a New Zealand writer, based in Auckland. His short comedies have been produced on four continents from New York and London to Sydney and Chennai.
    Website: https://www.rexmcgregor.com/

Adrian Miller is an avid traveler, theater fanatic, amateur photographer, owner of 3 businesses, wife, mom, and grandmom, and has never turned down a slice of pizza or a glass of red wine, especially when they are offered at the same time. Having been to Italy numerous times, Rome remains one of her favorite cities.

William John Rostron's books have a readership that spans four continents and all fifty states. His series of novels steeped in the 1960s music and culture, Band in the Wind, Sound of Redemption, and Brotherhood of Forever, have received critical acclaim from Writers Digest, the Online Book Club Review, and have consistently received Amazon ratings of 4.5 out of 5, or higher. He recently added to this series with The Other Side of the Wind, a book that may be read either independently of the series or in addition to it. He has published over three dozen short stories in anthologies, five receiving awards from Writers Digest in 2022. Many of these pieces appear in his short story compilation, A Flamingo Under the Carousel. Five of his stories s have been produced on the New York stage and are available for viewing on the author's website. Recently, he has finished work editing the Red Penguin anthology, KAPOW. www.WilliamJohn-Rostron.com

Born and raised in Queens, NY, William John Rostron now splits his time between his home on Long Island and traveling the country in his Tiffin motorhome. He is busy completing a bucket list of travel adventures when not writing. In the past 18 years, he and his wife, Marilyn, have traveled 140,000 miles. These journeys have taken them to the 48 contiguous states, 133 national parks, all 30 major league baseball stadiums, 154 cities and towns, two Canadian provinces, and various unusual experiences and locations. Many of these locations have served as backgrounds for his books.

He is presently working on a second book of short stories tentatively titled T-Rex Stole My Computer and a fifth novel, Dancing with the Lost.

www.WilliamJohnRostron.com

Lois Schaffer has devoted her energies as an activist, author, grant writer, for non-profit organizations, and the thrill to travel abroad.

Her activism includes rallies in support of the civil rights movement, equal rights, the freedom of choice and protests regarding the lack of gun safety measures.

Lois has published articles on the gun issue in addition to two books, "The Unthinkable: Life, Loss and a Mother's Mission to Ban Illegal Guns," and "From Bullet to Bullhorn, Stories of Advocacy, Activism and Hope," the latter gratefully published by Red Penguin Books.

The opportunity to be included in this volume on Rome emphasizes her love for travel and most gratifying.

Karen Shaw was a stay-at-home mom and then forged a successful career in Print advertising. All this led her into the entrepreneurial world as founder/designer/storyteller at Picture This Photo Books, and storyteller with Story Time with Karen.

During those years she wrote several short stories and poems, but never submitted them, making this her first published piece. Karen has written so much more over these last years as the marketer for Picture This Photo Books and writer for Story Time with Karen. Due to all this exposure, her confidence in her writing grew and when this opportunity arose, she went for it.

Rachel Abraham, the other half of this duo, has shown herself to be an amazing writer. She and Karen have collaborated on several written pieces over the years and found they worked extremely well together.

MEET OUR CONTRIBUTORS

Since this trip was theirs, they not only collaborated on the story, they agreed to submit it and see what happens.

The trip itself was a dream come true, and to raise it even higher, their story, Karen (aka Grandma) and Rachel's Italian Adventure, is now published.

Jim Tritten is a retired Navy carrier pilot who lives in a semi-rural New Mexico village. He is the Military Writers Society of America (MWSA) 2023 Writer of the Year and the recipient of the 2023 Parris Award from SouthWest Writers.

Janet Metz Walter has been writing since elementary school where she had several articles appear in the school literary journal.

Her first published book is "The 2 Carrot Ring and Other Fascinating Jewelry Stories, " a collection of stories contributed by a variety of people about the stories behind their own personal jewelry inspired by her family business. Janet also does interactive programs for groups about the book and members own personal stories.

Since then, she has contributed stories to several Red Penguin anthologies.

Among her many vocations and activities, Janet spent many years as a travel, agent, and world traveler and is thrilled to have contributed to several of the travel anthologies , and to this book on Rome.

Patricia Walkow is an award-winning author of newspaper and magazine articles, short stories, and full-length works of fiction and narrative non-fiction. She is a curator, editor, and contributor to many anthologies, many of which have been recognized for excellence. Her most recent publications are Life Lessons from the Color Yellow, a philosophical memoir written as a collection of short stories, and Alchemy's Reach, a murder mystery with a touch of romance, set in New Mexico's southeastern Sacramento Mountains. Ms. Walkow is a member of SouthWest Writers, Corrales Writing Group, and the Military Writers Society of America. She lives in Corrales, New Mexico with her husband and pets.

James Weems is a writer who has a unique sense of humor and a world of experience.

A lifelong writer, he has written (and lost) dozens of poems, several short stories, and co-authored one play, which was published in the Library of Congress and promptly buried under a layer of dust. After all, a musical with a Welsh title isn't a big draw, right?

Fortunately, several poems and a few of his short stories were published in college literary magazines and an Atlanta publication, The Unknowns.

He is passionate about getting the characters of his first novel out of his brain and onto the page.

James lives in Avondale Estates, Georgia, the first "planned community" in the United States, with his editor-in-chief kitten, Angel.